The Conquistadors: A Very Short Introduction

VERY SHORT INTRODUCTIONS are for anyone wanting a stimulating
and accessible way in to a new subject. They are written by experts and have
been published in more than 25 languages worldwide.

The series began in 1995 and now represents a wide variety of topics in
history, philosophy, religion, science, and the humanities. The VSI library
now contains 300 volumes—a Very Short Introduction to everything from
ancient Egypt and Indian philosophy to conceptual art and cosmology—and
will continue to grow in a variety of disciplines.

Very Short Introductions available now:

Available soon:

For more information visit our web site

www.oup.co.uk/general/vsi/

Matthew Restall and Felipe Fernández-Armesto

THE
CONQUISTADORS

A Very Short Introduction

OXFORD
UNIVERSITY PRESS

Oxford University Press, Inc., publishes works that further
Oxford University's objective of excellence
in research, scholarship, and education.

Oxford New York
Auckland   Cape Town   Dar es Salaam   Hong Kong   Karachi
Kuala Lumpur   Madrid   Melbourne   Mexico City   Nairobi
New Delhi   Shanghai   Taipei   Toronto

With offices in
Argentina   Austria   Brazil   Chile   Czech Republic   France   Greece
Guatemala   Hungary   Italy   Japan   Poland   Portugal   Singapore
South Korea   Switzerland   Thailand   Turkey   Ukraine   Vietnam

Copyright © 2012 by Oxford University Press, Inc.

Published by Oxford University Press, Inc.
198 Madison Avenue, New York, NY 10016

www.oup.com

Library of Congress Cataloging-in-Publication Data
Restall, Matthew, 1964–
The conquistadors : a very short introduction /
Matthew Restall and Felipe Fernández-Armesto.
p.   cm.—(Very short introductions)
Includes bibliographical references and index.
ISBN 978-0-19-539229-6
1. America—Discovery and exploration—Spanish.
2. Latin America—History—To 1600.
3. Conquerors—Spain—History.
4. Conquerors—America—History.
I. Fernández-Armesto, Felipe. II. Title.
E123.R387   2011
970.01′5—dc22   2011014388

1 3 5 7 9 8 6 4 2

Printed in Great Britain
by Ashford Colour Press Ltd., Gosport, Hants.
on acid-free paper

Contents

List of illustrations

Preface

Conquests craft cultures. They project colonists, ideas, languages, religions, goods, foods, diseases, manners, and ways of life and thought across frontiers and between environments. They craft new states and create the arenas of exchange we call empires. They are typically deplorable—violent, disruptive, exploitative, subversive, destructive. They can also be creative and transforming. They are among history's most influential, most impactful processes. How and why they happen are among history's most perplexing, most puzzling problems. The events that turned the sixteenth-century Spanish monarchy into a vast, ocean-spanning empire of land and sea—the only empire of that scale and nature in its day—are exemplary, even paradigmatic, for historians of conquests.

Other European conquerors in the wider world tried to emulate and imitate the conquistadors. Students of empire-building have seen the Spanish endeavors, especially in Mexico and the Andean world, as models for describing and explaining the outcomes of encounters between invaders and indigenous peoples all over the world. This book aims to explain who the conquistadors were, what they did, how they did it, and how they thought and felt and behaved. It should become apparent, to readers who persevere, that most accounts misrepresent the conquistadors, mistake the nature of their achievement, and mislead the world.

We focus on the period from the first transatlantic voyage of Christopher Columbus in 1492 to the extinction of the Inca kingdom in Vilcabamba in 1572. The conquistadors were mostly Spaniards, men from the Iberian kingdoms that became Spain (notably Castile). Some women were involved in ways that claim attention. Black Africans—slaves and free men—also took part in conquests; those who fought alongside the European invaders we call "black conquistadors." They helped make possible permanent Spanish settlements in the Americas and in rare cases founded kingdoms of their own. Even more influential and helpful in the creation of the Spanish empire were Native Americans who cooperated with the invaders; those who fought as Spaniards' allies we call "indigenous" or "native conquistadors."

Acknowledgments

We are grateful to Susan Ferber at Oxford University Press for the opportunity to write this book and for her many editorial contributions. Matthew Restall would like to thank Felipe Fernández-Armesto for his willingness to collaborate on the project; it was Felipe who introduced Matthew as an undergraduate at Oxford to the conquistadors, so this collaboration has special meaning to him. Felipe would like to echo the sentiments: it is thrilling for a teacher to see a beloved student become an admired colleague. We are also grateful to the outside readers who offered useful comments on earlier drafts. Finally, we thank the students of Matthew Restall's Penn State undergraduate seminar, "The Conquistadors" (Fall 2009), for their many contributions on paper and in class to the development of this book; in particular Andrew Barsom, Nicholas Borsuk, Matthew Bullington, Ayren Erickson, Taner Gokce, Lisa Hutton, Alison Hunt, Ryan Miller, Heather Parks, Blaire Patrick, and Hannah Tracy.

Chapter 1
A great many hardships

"We endured a great many hardships on the journey to this new kingdom," wrote Diego Romero, a veteran conquistador, "as much from having to slash new paths through the mountains and hills, as from hunger and sickness. And we arrived in this kingdom naked and barefoot, burdened by the weight of our own weapons, all of which caused the deaths of large numbers of Spaniards." The expedition Romero described was the Spanish invasion in 1536–39 of the indigenous lands that would become the heartland of Colombia. We know little about Romero but more about the leader of the expedition, Gonzalo Jiménez de Quesada. Our opening questions are, therefore, how typical were complaints like Romero's, and what kind of man was Jiménez de Quesada?

Was Jiménez de Quesada cruel and rapacious? A thief and murderer? Could we call him a sociopath? Or was he a family man, seeking advancement and a way to support his dependents, taking advantage of the opportunities of the day? His official mission was "to discover and pacify" new lands; can we allow that he was simply following orders in his "pacification" of the Native Americans he encountered, or must we highlight the irony of a term used to characterize what Spaniards in the same breath called "conquest and colonization"? Can we better understand him as a medieval figure, a manifestation on American soil of old Iberian traditions of religious warfare, or an

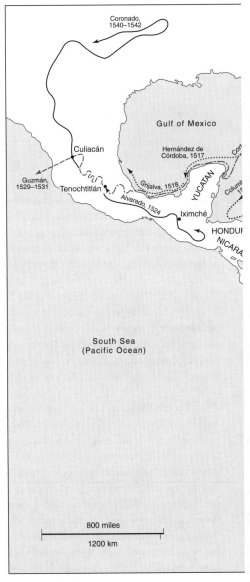

1. The Americas of the conquistadors.

early modern man, an explorer and conqueror in the genesis of the era of global empires?

In 1536 Jiménez de Quesada was hard at work in the Spanish colonial port city of Santa Marta, on the Caribbean coast of today's Colombia (see fig. 1). The twenty-seven-year-old Spaniard was the newly appointed leader of an expedition of discovery into the Colombian interior to find the source of the Magdalena River and thereby a route to Peru and the Pacific—the "South Sea." A few years before, Spaniards had invaded the Inca Empire, and word of the gold and silver discovered there had spread rapidly back to Spain. A lawyer by training, Jiménez de Quesada's initial task was an administrative one: to retain the services of some eight hundred Spaniards, brought from the Canary Islands not with offers of a salary but on the mere promise of future spoils; he had to determine which six hundred would march into the unknown by land, and which two hundred would sail up the Magdalena River; and he had to organize hundreds of African slaves and thousands of native American slaves and servants to carry equipment, forage and cook, spy and interpret, and—if necessary—fight for the Spaniards.

It took the expedition a year to reach the high plains and valleys of Colombia's interior. Only a quarter of the Spaniards—Jiménez de Quesada himself and 196 others—survived the journey. The rest died from malnutrition and starvation, infection and illness—the hardships described by Diego Romero. The mortality rate among African and native slaves and auxiliaries was not recorded.

The survivors emerged into a different world. For the next two years they lived among the Muisca, the people to whom the highland valleys were home. Very few of the surviving Spaniards died, none of them in military encounters. The Muisca were not politically centralized (there was no Muisca empire like that of the Aztecs in Mexico or Inca in Peru), so Jiménez de Quesada was able to play off Muisca leaders against each other and establish

4

some living space for the invaders. The local natives sustained the Spaniards, who meanwhile gathered some 200,000 pesos' worth of gold and close to two thousand emeralds. Eventually, Jiménez de Quesada founded three municipalities, named Santa Fé (today's Bogotá), Tunja, and Vélez.

For those two years, having no contact with the outside world, Jiménez de Quesada acted as an independent warlord. He was a diplomat, forging and breaking alliances, outwitting rivals, and bullying subordinates. He was a military leader, organizing raids, defending territory, capturing and torturing enemy chiefs. He was an administrator, seizing and dividing spoils, managing the multiracial settlers for whom he was responsible, making laws, founding towns, recording his actions on paper. He had, in effect, become king of highland Colombia in all but name. But his intention was never to rule an independent kingdom. Ever mindful that his license had been to explore and discover, not conquer and settle, he had his deeds notarized in the hope that Spain's King Charles would recognize his personal sacrifices and reward his loyalty with the granting of a governorship. His personal goal was not to lead a life of exploration and conquest, nor to lead his own army or rule his own fiefdom; it was to administer a pacified province of the empire, as a man of wealth and status, a manager and judge of men. His was the grand ambition of a sixteenth-century lawyer.

Jiménez de Quesada was, in short, a conquistador.

Mythmakers

Gonzalo Jiménez de Quesada is not as famous as Hernando Cortés or Francisco Pizarro; the Muisca are not as well known as the Aztecs and Inca. Jiménez de Quesada did not write artful letters to the king, as did Cortés, nor did one of his men pen a stirring account of the expedition to rival Bernal Díaz del Castillo's telling of the invasion of Mexico. Even in his own lifetime, Jiménez de

2. A portrait of Gonzalo Jiménez de Quesada. This 1886 etching of the conqueror of Colombia is based on colonial-period portraits: the facial features and pale beard match sixteenth-century depictions of Jiménez de Quesada; the half-length, three-quarter view, arm on parapet, is characteristic of early modern portraits; the armor and helmet evoke military status. Despite his wealth and high local standing as a veteran conquistador, reflected in this image, Jiménez de Quesada remained bitter over his denial of the governorship of the province.

Quesada complained bitterly that he had acquired more wealth for the Crown than Cortés and Pizarro, who "did not discover or settle better or richer provinces than I, even if the lands they conquered were larger." Nor was he given his just rewards, he felt, either in terms of reputation or official position. When two other Spanish expeditions arrived in Muisca territory in 1539, Jiménez de Quesada traveled to Spain to make his case for the governorship; but after years of litigation, it was given to Santa Marta's governor, based on a legal technicality (see fig. 2).

Not despite his relative lack of fame but because of it, Jiménez de Quesada is a better candidate to introduce this book. Although the oft-told feats of Cortés and Pizarro will appear in the pages that follow, our volume is more about men like Jiménez de Quesada, a man of middling status, higher ranked than the vast majority of Spaniards but not a nobleman. He was literate and educated but no man of letters. He sought opportunity in the New World at a time when dreams of success on the other side of the ocean were hardly original for a man who could afford the journey. He was in his late twenties during the main expedition of his life, a typical age for such an experience. He was lucky to survive, seeing most of the men he led die of disease, starvation, or battle wounds—not just the six hundred who perished in 1536–37, but the almost five hundred Spaniards, hundreds of Africans, and fifteen hundred natives who did not survive his 1569–72 expedition into eastern Colombia.

Jiménez de Quesada's greatest achievement, finding the Muisca and their lands, was followed not by a Crown-appointed governorship of the region for many years but by a dozen years of litigation and political frustration in Spain. Here again his experience was typical. The Crown controlled conquistadors by wrapping them in legal red tape. He spent the rest of his life petitioning for funds and rewards, and complaining of the unjust lack thereof. The tone of such protestations was central to the way conquistadors were expected to write of their deeds so must be taken with large amounts of salt. Yet some conquistadors, Jiménez de Quesada among them, seemed to internalize the badly-done-by-culture more than others. Later in life, out of frustration, he sought to repeat past triumphs with a new expedition, one destined to fail miserably and leave him to die in debt—as he did in 1579, at the age of seventy.

But the story of the Spanish conquistadors was not to be written by or about the likes of Jiménez de Quesada. Indeed, as he himself churlishly recognized, the core narrative had already been penned and published by the time he was pacing the halls of the Spanish court in the 1540s.

That story originated in the reports that the earliest conquistadors were obliged to send back to the king in Spain. Conquistadors were not soldiers in a royal army dispatched to the New World by the king. They went on their own initiative, assembling investors and companies of men with considerable individual effort and ingenuity. They were, in short, armed entrepreneurs. In some cases, the king himself was an investor in a company. But typically the only royal support that a conquistador carried with him into the unknown was a piece of paper—the most important such document being a license to invade and conquer, making the holder an *adelantado* (a medieval military title, literally "advance man," meaning "invader"). A successful, surviving adelantado had a good shot at being appointed governor of a new province within a Spanish American kingdom. Yet even an adelantado had to submit an extensive series of reports detailing his activities.

All conquistadors had to submit reports to the king—from renowned adelantados and other captains down to the humblest Spanish, Native American, and black African conquerors. These reports described the services, merits, and sacrifices of the author, offered up to the court as justification for royal favor in the form of offices, titles, and pensions. The genre was therefore called the *probanza de mérito*, or proof of merit.

The purpose of the probanza determined its style, its tone, and the evolution of its conventions to encompass almost all conquistador literature. Individual action and achievement were privileged at the expense of collective process and pattern, promoting the notion that victories came through the glorious deeds of great men. The genre also helped to fan the flames of the factionalism and violent rivalries that characterized the conquest era, as each probanza author attempted to sell his own merits to the king and dismiss or denigrate competing conquistadors.

Similarly, the roles played by non-Spaniards were systematically marginalized. Black Africans and men of mixed race, both slaves and free, fought in every company and often played key roles. Blacks often operated independently, forging their own little states and kingdoms, sometimes in collaboration with natives, rather as Spaniards did on a larger scale: their exploits show that it was not necessary to be white, or to have European resources in order to achieve power in parts of the early modern New World. In most conquests native auxiliaries greatly outnumbered Spaniards and preceded them in battle. But conquistador writings downplay the very existence of the non-Spanish participants, let alone the crucial nature of their presence.

Finally, conquistadors were always eager to show that they were not only loyal servants of the king but good Christians. That concept was particularly significant for Iberians at the turn of the sixteenth century, as the peninsula had experienced many centuries of the coexistence of three religions—Christianity, Islam, and Judaism. That coexistence had always been a complex mixture of harmonious and hostile, peaceful and violent. But conflict became increasingly prevalent, so that by the 1490s a series of persecutions led to the exile or forced conversion of Jews, while the last Muslim kingdom fell to the sword of the Christian kingdoms of Castile and Aragon in 1492.

During the sixteenth century, the "good Christian" Spanish world faced two new threats: Protestantism and the forms of paganism that Spanish explorers, missionaries, traders, and warriors encountered in the wider world. Thus, not surprisingly, conquistadors were quick to echo arguments that originated in the narratives of the conquests from clerical and courtly propagandists: their campaigns in the Americas were divinely guided and sanctioned. Providence had chosen Castilians to unite Iberia under Christianity, and then to bring Christianity to the heathens of the New World. The conquistadors succeeded "by a miracle of God," as Gaspar Marquina, a conquistador in Peru, put it. In a letter back to his father in Spain he asserted that hundreds of thousands of Andean natives had been converted, and that the tiny company of Spaniards had taken the Inca emperor, Atahualpa, only because "God gave us the victory miraculously over him and his forces." The frequently attested presence on battlefields of apparitions of the Blessed Virgin or of St. James the Apostle did not detract from individual conquistadors' claims to the rewards due to prowess: on the contrary, they demonstrated divine favor, an obvious fact the king could surely not ignore.

As well as providentialism and the rhetoric of petitions for reward, a third set of literary conventions distorted the writings of conquistadors and, therefore, the historiographical tradition. Most conquistador writers shared a background as readers of the sixteenth-century equivalent of airport-bookstall fiction: romances of chivalry, in which a hero, destined for greatness but down on his luck, takes to a life of adventure, battles monsters or giants or pagans, and ends up conquering an island or ruling a kingdom (and, in a common fade-out, marrying a princess). These stories inspired the conquistadors, providing plotlines and imagery for their lives and how they wrote about them.

The combination of these conventions, together with the awkward realities of operations in hostile, remote, and unfamiliar environments, produced paradoxes within conquistador literature. On the one hand, conquests were providential; on the other, they were individual. On the one hand, they were miraculous; and on the other, procured by conquistadors' heroism. On the one hand they fulfilled a collective Spanish destiny of triumph in dilating the frontiers of the faith; on the other, they were the work of collaborators whose allegiance hardly took account of Spain, for the very concepts of "Spain" and "Spaniards" only gradually cohered and spread during the sixteenth century among the disparate and conflictive peoples and nations that made up the Spanish monarchy.

On the one hand, Spaniards found immensely rich lands, overflowing with precious metals and with industrious natives who could easily be turned into tribute-paying Christians. Conquistador leaders writing early reports usually made such claims. And yet, on the other hand, the extraction of these riches and pacification of the local peoples seldom proved easy, requiring the extension of more credit, the acquisition of more support and supplies, and the promise of greater royal favors. As a result, conquistadors often made premature claims of victory while requesting help in completing a conquest still in its genesis.

On the one hand, conquistadors made much of their great deeds and extraordinary successes. They trumpeted their triumphs not just to the king but in letters to relatives and patrons, and in versions of their probanzas and letters that the better-connected conquistadors were able to publish. On the other hand, conquistador accounts are packed with complaints, sufferings, and sacrifices. Conquest was a dangerous and miserable business that left its practitioners impoverished and in pain, at the mercy of the king's pity.

The characteristics of the probanzas, dictated and written in the Americas and sent to the king in Spain, spilled over immediately into related genres of writing. Similar types of reports were *cartas* (letters), *relaciones* (accounts), or *cartas de relación*. The lines between private letters, official correspondence, and public letters composed for publication, were blurred. Royal officials penned a "letter" from Columbus to be sent to the presses months after

3. The white horses of Hernando Cortés. In a scene from a Conquest of Mexico *biombo* now in the Franz Mayer Museum in Mexico City (*this page*), Cortés and his men are depicted anachronistically as seventeenth-century soldiers, with Cortés's pose on a rearing white horse intended to evoke the Moor-slaying saint, Santiago (*opposite page*, shown in this 1610 bas relief by Miguel Mauricio). The biombo (from the Japanese *byobu*), a decoratively painted set of 4 to 20 folding screens, was introduced into Mexico by the Japanese embassy in 1614 and was a popular medium into the mid-eighteenth century for portraying conquistador achievements.

the Genoese had returned from his first Atlantic crossing. The relaciones of Cortés to the king, which amounted to an elaborate and cleverly crafted probanza, sold so well in published form in Cortés's lifetime that the king had them banned. Pedro de Alvarado had his letters to Cortés, promoting his conquest of Guatemala, published in Spain while Alvarado was still in Guatemala struggling desperately against the Maya. Bernal Díaz wrote a series of probanzas, each with little success, each longer than the previous one, until his final version became a vast account of the Spanish conquests in Mexico and Central America—published after his death as a six-hundred-page book and still widely read today.

By this time (Díaz's *True History* came out in 1632), the conventions of conquistador literature had hardened into a conventional narrative, one given official sanction and perpetuated by successive royal chroniclers. The post of *coronista* or *cronista del rey* ("royal chronicler") had been created in the 1450s, became prestigious under Ferdinand and Isabella, and led to the writing of ever-larger accounts of Spanish triumphs—especially conquistador exploits—in the sixteenth and seventeenth centuries. Parallel to the "truth" claims of conquistador letters and reports, royal chronicles paradoxically laid claim to objective veracity while also insisting that their perspective was that of a royal official glorifying the Crown. "My job is to tell the truth," stated cronista Tomás Tamayo de Vargas in 1639. But only a royal chronicler could be trusted to write "with the truth and clarity that is required," as Gonzalo Fernández de Oviedo put it; he saw his role as that of an "evangelist" whose mission was to immortalize the glories of Spain's conquistadors and kings, a concept surely rooted in the providential presumptions of the likes of Cortés. Royal chroniclers perpetuated myths rooted in conquistadors' own self-aggrandizing claims. In the seventeenth century the efforts of the coronistas del rey to promote the conquistadors in print were paralleled in paint. Conquest paintings in various forms and sizes came into vogue—the most striking being that of the *biombo* (see fig. 3)—all projecting the conventional conquistador narrative.

God sometimes operated directly or through the saints, particularly Santiago, popularly depicted on his white horse with Iberian Muslims or Moors crushed beneath its hooves; the claim that the saint was seen coming to the rescue of Spaniards against Aztecs in 1520, and again saving conquistadors from Inca during the 1537 siege of Cuzco, was repeated until it became part of the grand narrative of the conquest. By the seventeenth century, paintings of Cortés in battle often turned him into a Santiago avatar (as fig. 3 illustrates).

At other times, especially in versions conquistadors wrote or controlled themselves, God operated through his agents, the Spaniards themselves. In his letters to the king, Cortés explained that victory was made possible by a combination of divine providence and the courage of the conquistadors. "God gave us such a victory," he wrote, but also "we killed many people." The brave Spaniards, he noted, "dare face the greatest peril, consider fighting their glory, and have the habit of winning." Francisco López de Gómara, chaplain and biographer to Cortés in his twilight years, exclaimed that "Spaniards are most worthy of praise in all parts of the world. Blessed be God who gave them such grace and power."

The circularity of the conquistador argument was irresistible: the triumph of the conquistadors proved that God was on their side, and they prevailed because of God's will; their invasions and conquests in the New World were justified by God's support, and Spaniards knew they had such support because they were able to defeat their enemies.

Precedents

Before we turn in more detail to the conquistadors of the sixteenth century, we must answer two questions. What happened in the Americas that determined what Europeans would find there? And what had Europeans being doing before the 1490s that led them to the Americas in that decade?

Mesoamericans and Andeans tended to settle in fertile valleys or on high plateaus, rather than in heavily forested areas. There they built villages, towns, and sometimes cities, sustained by permanent, intensive agriculture. Complex food production and the urban concentration of people facilitated social stratification and economic specialization. Spanish explorers and conquistadors deliberately sought sedentary societies. In the short run, they could not survive without them. In the long run, it was dense native settlements, agricultural productivity, recognizable hierarchies, and tax-paying systems that made Spanish colonies possible.

The Aztec and Inca empires rose more or less simultaneously. According to traditional but insecure chronologies, the Nahuatl-speaking Mexica took control of much of the Valley of Mexico in 1428, the key foundational event in the genesis of the Aztec Empire; and a Quechua prince seized power in 1438 and began to turn the Inca kingdom into an empire—the greatest that the Americas had ever seen. Both processes probably started later than tradition claimed. The two empires grew rapidly, and by the time that Columbus made his first voyage across the Atlantic in 1492, they dominated central Mexico and the Andes, respectively.

Aztec ideology of empire was interwoven with religious ideas and beliefs. The ritual execution of war captives and other carefully chosen victims had been practiced in Mesoamerican societies for thousands of years, but in the fifteenth century the Aztecs appear to have taken human sacrifice to new levels, both in terms of meaning and scale. Huitzilopochtli, the patron god of war and of the imperial capital, was the divine audience for the killing of war captives, who typically had their hearts removed and their heads placed on the skull rack in the plaza of Tenochtitlán—the spectacular Aztec capital on an island in the center of Lake Texcoco. To a lesser extent, other Nahuas (Nahuatl-speaking peoples of central Mexico) also embraced this culture of ritualized violence. The Tlaxcalans, for example, who had always resisted the Aztec Empire that surrounded their city and its lands, likewise cut out the hearts of prisoners of war. Tlaxcala remained independent, but its life was overshadowed in numerous ways by the existence of Aztec hegemony across central Mexico, breeding generations of resentment that would prove crucial to the outcome of the Spanish invasion.

From 1502 until his murder by Spanish invaders in 1520, the Aztec paramount, Moctezuma Xocoyotl, aggressively consolidated his authority and extended the empire of his ancestors. Long after his death, both Spaniards and natives unfairly blamed him for the destruction of his empire. In fact, the arrival of Spaniards set loose a chain of events beyond Moctezuma's control; for the previous eighteen years he had been an exceptionally successful leader, increasing the authority and influence of the empire more than any of his predecessors.

At around the same time that the Aztec Empire was being forged, something similar was being achieved thousands of miles to the south. In 1438, by traditional reckoning, Cusi Yupanqui, a secondary prince in the Inca kingdom, crushed an attempt by the neighboring Chanca kingdom to annex the Inca heartland centered on Cuzco. This victory prompted him to force his father into retirement and seize the throne—to put it in Inca terms, *maskapaycha* or fringed crown—from its designated heir. Yupanqui also renamed himself Pachacuti, meaning Earthquake, or World-Changer. He changed the world by recasting the past, present, and future: the past was cast as preparation for Pachacuti's arrival (even the Chanca threat may have been manufactured by Pachacuti as a pretext for his power play); the present was the context for a reorganization of the Inca political system to legitimize Pachacuti's rule and accommodate the administrative demands of the new empire; and the future was conceived as a succession of campaigns to bring Inca civilization to all the other Andean peoples.

Whereas the Aztec Empire covered a relatively modest 100,000 square miles, and included enclaves of unconquered city-states, the Inca Empire covered a vast contiguous region that stretched 2,600 miles from Ecuador to Chile, sandwiched between Amazonia and the Pacific. We call the empire after its ruler ("Sapa Inca" was the emperor's title), but it was Quechua peoples based in Cuzco who created the empire, which they called Tawantinsuyu, the Land of the Four Quarters.

Like the Aztecs, the Inca expanded their empire though a combination of military conquest, threats of military action, and alliance building. But whereas the Aztecs emphasized indirect rule and tribute collection, the Inca involved themselves more closely in the lives of subject peoples, establishing networks of power with subordinate elites through marriages, ritual ties, hostage-taking, military alliances, and the exchange of cults, as well through such obvious techniques as war and terror. They practiced what might best be called "ecological imperialism," shifting goods and labor between the vast array of climatic zones the Andean world comprised. The system was traditional among Andean empires, but the Inca carried it to new lengths, as they united territories more extensive and more diverse than ever before. Unlike the Aztecs, they focused on extracting labor rather than tribute payment in goods, although both were important. Under the imperial labor system, called the *mit´a* (literally "turn," an ancient term preserved under Spanish rule), local farmers worked lands appropriated by the Inca state as well as their own lands, while men took turns serving in the Inca armies and on urban construction sites. There was a labor rotation system in central Mexico, called *coatequitl* (literally "snake-work"), but it was not manipulated at an imperial state level.

The mita also provided labor for the building of an extensive 14,000-mile network of royal roads. In form these ranged from wide highways to rope suspension bridges spanning mountain gorges, permitting royal llama herds and relay runners, armies and tribute goods to be moved up and down the empire. The road system, unique in the Americas, tied together a chain of warehouses that stored food, textiles, and other goods, all of which supplied armies, fed mita workers, and maintained the wealthy Inca elite. The Inca also used *quipus* (rows of colored, knotted cords) to store tribute information and convey messages. The two rulers who succeeded Pachacuti, his son Topa Inca and grandson Huayna Capac, continued the policy of nonstop campaigns. As the empire spread, so did its system of roads, garrisons, warehouses, labor control, and rapid communication through runners and quipus.

Sometime in the late 1520s, Huayna Capac died suddenly, probably from smallpox, which spread from Mexico faster than the Spaniards. The disease claimed both him and shortly afterwards his chosen heir—before a single Spaniard set foot in the Inca Empire. The throne then fell to a minor, Manco, whose two brothers, Atahualpa and Huascar, agreed to share rule of the empire. That arrangement disintegrated into civil war within a couple of years. The Spaniards were lucky; they arrived in 1532, while the Inca were temporarily divided. Had they invaded later, they likely would have found one of Huayna Capac's sons firmly in control of the empire.

The similarity between what were in effect the Aztec and Inca imperial charters is coincidence; the two empires developed independently and were not aware of each other's existence. Some scholars have tried to explain the success of the conquistadors in terms of the weakness of the Aztec and Inca empires, arguing that both had peaked by the 1520s. But neither the empires nor their emperors were fragile and enfeebled when the Spaniards arrived; on the contrary, Moctezuma was poised to expand his domain into Maya country, and Atahualpa was poised to consolidate control over his vast domain.

Beyond the empires of the Aztecs and Inca, Spaniards encountered societies sedentary and urbanized in varying degrees (but politically less centralized). They sought to turn imperfectly sedentary communities—and, in the long term, even peoples with transhumant or nomadic ways of life—into sedentary colonial subjects. This process was typically violent but ultimately successful, at least from the Spanish perspective. Nonsedentary peoples, however, were largely able to resist conquest and incorporation into the new colonies for decades, if not centuries. They lived in the driest or wettest regions of the Americas. In general, sedentary Andeans such as the Inca and Muisca, and sedentary Mesoamericans such as the Aztecs and Maya, viewed neighboring forest, desert, and mountain peoples as barbarians whose dictary and other customs were despicable. Spaniards agreed. Such hostile feelings were mutual.

By their ways of life and their ideological prejudices, some native cultures were more disposed to sympathy with the Spaniards than others. But in all cases, the relationship between Spaniards and natives began on terms of utter mutual ignorance. The complete mutual isolation of Europe and Native America can be difficult for us to imagine, but there can be no doubt that for most of history, the Americas had little or no impact on the societies that developed in the rest of the world, while the rest of the world had little or no impact on Native Americans.

There remains some controversy over when migration into the Americas ceased, or even if it ever really did. Vikings established a settlement on Newfoundland around 1000 CE, but it made no apparent impact on the development of Native American societies. Similarly, it is possible that European fishers or whalers worked off the North Atlantic coasts of the Americas in late medieval times. But even if there were such migrants, they left no cultural or physical traces among the Americans. While the pattern of winds and currents makes it highly unlikely that Native Americans crossed either the Pacific or Atlantic oceans, it is probable that minimal, sporadic migration into the hemisphere continued by sea from Asia.

In any case, the Americas remained effectively isolated. Not until the 1490s did practical, two-way routes of exchange become accessible across the Atlantic; in the Pacific, comparable developments were deferred until Spanish navigators found the ways to cross that vast ocean in the 1560s. In the case of the Atlantic, slow, barely documented improvements in shipping, rigging, and water storage preceded the breakthrough, making long-range navigation increasingly possible. A culture of seaborne adventurism, meanwhile, developed in parts of Atlantic-side Europe, reflected in the seaborne romances of chivalric derring-do that explorers, as well as conquistadors, read and imitated. In the 1480s Atlantic enterprise became profitable, as Portuguese entrepreneurs began to garner significant amounts of gold from West Africa. Meanwhile, sugar production took off in the Canary Islands, and North Atlantic products fell increasingly into the hands of English, Portuguese, and Flemish traders. As a result, financiers became willing to fund such enterprises as that of Columbus.

Conquistador culture matured over a longer period. At intervals in medieval Spain, especially in the mid-thirteenth century, warfare gradually created a Muslim-Christian frontier that nudged southward. By 1264 the only Muslim kingdom left in the peninsula was Granada; it was whittled down in size by the most aggressive Christian kingdom, Castile, until falling completely in 1492. Castile was the largest and most populous kingdom in the peninsula; with five million inhabitants, it was five times larger than Portugal and Aragon. The pairing through marriage of the crowns of Castile and Aragon in 1479, the long conquest of the Canary Islands culminating in the 1490s, and the conquest of Granada helped to inculcate dynamic, imperial expectations and create a warrior mentality, attuned to war as a profession and spoils as rewards.

By the time of the discovery of the Caribbean islands, Castilian nobles, and those who aspired to nobility, expected that Castile would continue to be the dominant kingdom in an expanding imperium of kingdoms; that community of interests and sentiments between church and Crown would give Castilians the right to subdue, convert, and rule other peoples—rights papal approval confirmed; that the empire would be Christian in an aggressively exclusionist manner, at best converting Muslims, Jews, and Native Americas, at worst persecuting, enslaving, and slaughtering them; that the land or, at least, some of the labor and tribute of conquered peoples would be divided up among the conquering elite; and that the Castilian elite in conquered lands would live in cities, sustained by labor and produce from the surrounding countryside.

"Roman Spain was a world full of cities," the historian Michael Kulikowski has observed, "shaped by its hundreds of urban territories." This was true more than a thousand years later. Juan Pablo Mártir Rizo, a seventeenth-century Spanish humanist and historian, wrote that Castile was "a kingdom made of cities." The city was an increasingly complex locus of church and state power, elite wealth and status, Catholic civilization, and conquest and colonization. Seville in the sixteenth century was the largest, and arguably most multiracial, city in Europe. Likewise, Spanish cities in the Americas rapidly developed into mixed-race, multiethnic, polyglot environments—the genesis of which was the conquistador household, complete with its African and Native American subordinates. In short, the Spanish city, in Iberia and in the Americas, became the brand—the characteristic, defining feature—of the world wrought by the conquistadors.

The investors who backed Columbus lost most of their money. In the long run, however, their business sense turned out to be reliable. There were enormous profits to be made from perilous voyages into the Atlantic. Profits from West African gold and slaves, from Indian Ocean freighting opportunities, from Japanese silver, from southeast Asian spices, and from American precious metals and indigenous tribute payments would pay for European imperial expansion. In Portuguese and Dutch outreach across the oceans, commercial and conquistador attitudes were finely balanced: the makers of empires and settlers of frontiers were commonly merchants or peddlers or shippers by vocation, and sometimes "warrior merchants" who incarnated mercantile and bellicose values simultaneously. Yet despite the importance of trade and of sophisticated, multiracial urban culture in the making of the Spanish empire, in the Americas Castile's ethos of legalistic violence and colonization dominated the way conquistadors behaved.

By way of illustration, we return to Jiménez de Quesada in the high plains of Colombia. There the Spaniards had killed the Muisca ruler, Bogotá, and entered into an alliance with his successor, Sagipa. The Muisca lord agreed to "fill a small house with Bogotá's gold" (according to an anonymous Spanish account of 1545). But after a few days the Spaniards, dissatisfied with the amount and quality of metal delivered, begged Jiménez de Quesada "to place Sagipa in irons and have him tortured." When he refused, the conquistadors accused him of making a secret deal on the side with Sagipa. With the inevitable resort to violence hanging in the air, the conquistador-lawyers squared off against each other: the dissidents assigned one of their number, Jerónimo de Ayusa, to argue their case; and Jiménez de Quesada appointed his brother, Hernán Pérez de Quesada, to defend his position.

The semblance of due legal process could not spare the Muisca ruler. After arguing over the matter, "the Christians proceeded to torture Sagipa in order to compel him to hand over Bogotá's gold and confess where he had hidden it." Bound tightly, he was subjected to various torments, including having his feet burned and boiling animal fat poured on his chest. "In the end," states the anonymous Spanish account with a chilling succinctness, "Sagipa died."

Chapter 2
Many victories, great conquests

"It is because of wealth that we have witnessed, and will continue to see many victories, great conquests and discoveries of great empires that have been hidden from us," wrote the veteran conquistador and colonial administrator Bernardo de Vargas Machuca. "This is seen each day, under commanders who, with royal powers, have thus occupied themselves, with desire to show themselves serving their king and embarking on campaigns of great risk, labor, and expense, spending their personal wealth with no one else's help."

Included in his book, *The Indian Militia and Description of the Indies*, first published in 1599, such comments promoted the legendary narrative of self-sufficient yet supremely loyal conquistadors, whose sacrifices led inevitably to triumph. Vargas Machuca's arguments were propaganda, part of his defense of the conquistador. He knew only too well that the previous century had seen an abundance of disloyalty, graft, and failure—beginning with the unfortunate Caribbean experiment.

The Castilians had not been seeking a new world any more than the Portuguese had. Columbus's contract with the Castilian Crown was for the sea route to Asia; the Genoese insisted he had found it, but his claims could not resist critical scrutiny for long. When the Portuguese finally rounded Africa and pioneered the real sea route to Asia, the Castilian monarchs had Columbus arrested. He would make more Atlantic crossings, but he had become marginalized to the Castilian experiment in the Caribbean.

That experiment reflected the lessons of the long conquest of the Canary Islands. The financiers who backed Columbus came together as investors in the Canaries. The policies of nurturing and converting the native populations and exempting them from enslavement took shape in the archipelago. The ideas of introducing new crops, especially sugar, and importing labor to grow and process them, arose there. The establishment of the Canaries as a distinct "kingdom" within the Crown of Castile and the wider Spanish monarchy presaged the way Spaniards would conceive and organize the New World.

By 1500 the original settlements made by Columbus on Hispaniola were abandoned and a permanent Spanish capital established at Santo Domingo. Over the next twenty years, Spaniards used the stepping-stone method to explore, raid, and partially settle the islands of the Caribbean. After Hispaniola the other larger islands—Cuba, Puerto Rico, Jamaica—became bases for further small expeditions. Had the goal been to displace the indigenous population, extract mineral wealth, and return to Spain, the Caribbean years would have been deemed successful. But the goal was to forge a permanent and lucrative new kingdom of peaceful, hard-working, tribute-paying, Christian converts. By that token, the Caribbean experiment was a disaster.

The native Arawak or Taino peoples practiced agriculture, built permanent towns, and had complex social structures; but they also lived from hunting, fishing, and gathering, and their settlements were not in any sense cities. The Tainos were not used to rigorous labor systems, enforced by strict political and religious regimes, of the kinds long established in Iberia and soon to be found by Spaniards among the Aztecs and Inca. Spanish slaving raids and violence among the islanders produced further resistance, flight, and mortality—which in turn fostered greater frustration and counterproductive activities by Spaniards. Bartolomé de Las Casas claimed that the "egregious wickedness" of the colonists killed nine in ten of Hispaniola's Tainos. Although the Dominican friar ignored (or was ignorant of) the impact of epidemic disease, he was right that the island's population fell by 90 percent to perhaps around 15,000 people, by contemporary estimates, by around the middle of the second decade of the sixteenth century.

Led by priests such as Las Casas, the soul-searching began, while the Crown initiated criminal and policy investigations into why the Caribbean conquests were such disappointments. But long before such imperial self-reflection bore any fruit, the momentum of exploration and invasion took Spaniards to the mainland. There, the same methods would be employed, and the native population would likewise succumb to Old World diseases and decline catastrophically. In contrast to the Caribbean, there lay sprawling civilizations, the "great empires that have been hidden from us" (in Vargas Machuca's words), and millions of sedentary families— societies strong enough to survive the conquistador.

Two chains

As the Caribbean descended into a violent, low-profit disappointment, Spaniards began increasingly to explore the circum-Caribbean coastlines. Their discoveries there led to the forging of two great chains of conquest.

The first chain led from Cuba onto the Mexican mainland. Voyages of 1517 and 1518 explored and landed on the coast of the Yucatan peninsula, the closest mainland point to Cuba. The sponsor was the governor of Cuba, Diego Velázquez, who held the title of adelantado. Therefore when he commissioned one of the island's *encomenderos* (conquistador-settlers with rights to native labor and tribute) to lead a third expedition in 1519, he empowered the chosen leader, Hernando Cortés, to explore, not invade. The chain was thus a system of patronage, running from the king in Spain down to the lesser captains risking their lives at sea or in the jungles of the Americas; the link from jungle to court was not supposed to be direct, but paradoxically part of what made the chain strong were the continual attempts by Spaniards of lesser rank to grasp that chain and pull themselves closer to its royal source.

Suspecting that Cortés would attempt to do just that, bypassing his patronage and seeking direct royal support, Velázquez tried at the last minute, in vain, to stop the expedition sailing from Cuba. Once his five hundred men had landed on the Mexican mainland (via Cozumel and a quick sail along the Yucatec coast), Cortés grounded most of his eleven ships and formally declared direct allegiance to the king. He founded a city (a ritual act only), creating a town council whose votes of support lent a veneer of legality to his actions. It would be six years before Cortés would receive royal approval, in person in Spain, for his revolt against Velázquez and his war against the Aztecs.

The first Spanish invaders of Mexico moved slowly toward the capital city of what was—they were soon to discover—an impressive regional empire. They were few in number and ill equipped: their armor was an encumbrance (though steel swords were effective weapons, which had a remarkable impact in battle compared with the obsidian-studded clubs favored by native armies); their firearms and horses were few and of limited usefulness in the mountainous, city-studded terrain; and they had no means of renewing their supplies or munitions. They also had little chance to acclimatize to the almost unimaginable weather, environments, landscapes, foods, and diseases they encountered. And they were at the mercy of potential enemies who might have wiped them out, had they so wished.

So what saved them? Three circumstances: first, they were among peoples whose cultures predisposed them to receive strangers hospitably, and even with awe; second, they profited from the antagonisms between indigenous communities whose hatred of each other far outweighed any suspicions they might have felt toward the newcomers; third, it is arguable that most natives—while appreciating the newcomers as potential allies and esteeming them for the magic or sanctity their strangeness suggested—underestimated the threat they represented. Indigenous polities contended for Spanish friendship, offering gifts of food and women, and engaging in restrained forms of trial by combat to test their prowess and evaluate them as allies. Most notably the Tlaxcalans—the Aztecs´ principal rivals and foes—tested the conquistadors in battle and then appropriated them as allies, using them to assist in the massacre of hated neighbors in the city of Cholula.

Cortés thus found common ground with local lords. The Spaniards wanted to move on to the Valley of Mexico to confront the Aztec emperor with as many native allies as possible. Native rulers were eager to see the Spaniards leave their communities and were willing to hedge their bets on the possibility of the collapse of the Aztec Empire. Some, like the Totonacs, were subject to the Aztec Empire and quick to rebel against it. Others, like the Tlaxcalans, had resisted Aztec expansion and were eventually persuaded to take a chance on destroying their old enemies. The initiative in forging the alliance that eventually overthrew Aztec hegemony did not—could not—come from Cortés, who knew nothing of indigenous politics and could not speak any indigenous language. He relied on the native woman who acted as his interpreter, called doña Marina by Spaniards and Malinche by Nahuas. In native accounts of the conquest, she occupies a central role, at the very least a guiding and often a commanding one.

A combined force, in which Tlaxcalans and their own allies accompanied Spaniards, advanced toward Tenochtitlán. In November 1519 they entered the city as guests of Moctezuma. Conversing through Cortés's interpreter, the emperor delivered a welcoming speech to Cortés that the latter claimed to interpret (in a letter to the king) as a speech of surrender. Intrigued by these foreigners who had disrupted a corner of his empire, Moctezuma sought to display his majesty through hospitality. But the Spaniards, outnumbered and fearful, soon resorted to treachery and terror; in what was effectively a coup d´état, Cortés seized and imprisoned Moctezuma and ordered that anyone who so much as raised a hand against the Spanish and their allies be publicly cut to pieces and fed to the dogs. These were stock tactics developed by conquistadors in the course of their decades of Caribbean slave raiding, tactics that proved even more effective against mainland imperial peoples who depended on their divinely sanctioned kings. The use of terror was not only a workable strategy, it was also a psychological necessity for the tiny, beleaguered band of conquistadors, surrounded by unfamiliar perils and cut off from all hope of help from home.

Over the next eight months the Spanish and Tlaxcalan invaders, partially contained within the center of the city, survived, precariously and increasingly restively. Cortés continued to use displays of defiance and bravado to good effect. He ordered that images of the Virgin Mary be placed atop Aztec temples to assert the power of the invaders' god. He also took a contingent of Spaniards and native allies back to the Gulf Coast to confront a company of Velázquez supporters that had sailed from Cuba to challenge Cortés; they were defeated, and most joined Cortés, who returned to Tenochtitlán to find that the stalemate had shifted in favor of the Aztecs. Led by Pedro de Alvarado, the Spaniards were under siege.

The desperate Spaniards exhibited Moctezuma to the people. The gesture failed. The monarch died, murdered by the Spaniards or perhaps, as they later claimed, stoned to death by the mob. On the night of June 30, 1520, the invaders attempted to flee the city undetected. But Aztec warriors were waiting, and they killed about half the Spaniards and thousands of Tlaxcalan and other native allies. Cortés and his bedraggled Spanish forces eventually regrouped with Tlaxcalan assistance, but it would be more than a year before Tenochtitlán and its twin city of Tlatelolco fell. Cut off from the mainland, the Aztecs faced disease and starvation, then attack by land and water. Boats, built on the shores of Lake Texcoco and armed with cannon, policed the lake and helped pound remaining Aztec warrior contingents in canoes. The city was taken and pillaged, block by block, revealing not gold but piles of bodies, victims of sickness, starvation, and siege warfare. Even then, Cortés did not feel strong enough to proclaim the end of the Aztec world, but he tried to reassure incumbent elites, seeking a basis of accommodation with them and confirming Moctezuma's heir in the role of paramount. In and around the empire, however, people realized that the old days were over. In outlying areas, communities formerly cowed by the Aztecs resumed old rivalries and conflicts. The effect was to increase the Spaniards' power, since, as strangers uninvolved in traditional politics, they were much in demand as the arbitrators of disputes.

By the end of 1521, the old Aztec Empire was destroyed. But its framework of trade routes, tribute lists, and diplomatic relations between ruling families remained in place. Spaniards immediately sought to make use of that framework and convert it into an elemental part of the structure of their own empire in Mesoamerica—which they renamed the Kingdom of New Spain. In most communities, the Spaniards came to an understanding with existing elites, without any need for violence—a fact the historiographical tradition has ignored or suppressed, perhaps because of the conquistadors' misleading focus on their own prowess. The Aztecs had themselves employed a chain of conquest in the region. The Spaniards used that chain—and even used Aztec warriors, survivors of the war who joined other Nahua allies—to expand the frontiers of New Spain. In the 1520s, just as Mexico City began to rise, reconstructed with a fresh look in a new, Spanish-inspired style, from the rubble of Tenochtitlán, so did a new Spanish-Mexican empire spring from the ashes of the old empire of the Mexica.

Cortés himself led an expedition to Honduras (taking the opportunity to confirm the displacement of power into his own hands by executing the last Aztec emperor, the captive Cuauhtémoc, on the way). Honduras was more or less conquered in the 1530s by Francisco de Montejo, who also led companies into the Yucatan peninsula, twice failing to conquer the Yucatec Maya; his son eventually founded a small colony there in the 1540s. Meanwhile, Pedro de Alvarado invaded highland Guatemala in 1524, leaving two years later with little to show but a legacy of violence. The chain of conquest led Spaniards quickly into most corners of Mesoamerica—and, soon after, north into what is today the U.S. Southwest, and west across the Pacific to what would be renamed the Philippines. But the founding of colonies would prove to be a protracted and highly contested process. The material and political conquest of the Mesoamerican center had not been easy, and at the fringes the conquest would take centuries. Equally challenging would be the winning of the hearts and minds of millions of former Aztec subjects and other native groups who were officially subjects of the king of Spain. This would be the long story of colonial Mesoamerica, a "New Spain" so unlike its Iberian namesake.

If one sequence of conquest ran from Hispaniola to Cuba to Mexico to Central America, another extended from Hispaniola to the Isthmus of Panama—and from there down the Pacific side of South America. The conquest and settlement of a small colony on the Atlantic side of the isthmus began in 1508, and five years later Panama received the first Spanish bishop appointed to the mainland of the Americas. That same year, the Pacific side of the isthmus was discovered by an African slave and his owner, Vasco Núñez de Balboa—the first sighting of the Pacific Ocean by invaders from the Old World.

During the next decade, Spaniards established a settlement on the Pacific side (named Panama) and began to explore the coast and ocean to its south (which Spaniards called the South Sea). Among the early settlers on the isthmus were the Pizarro brothers. One of them, Francisco, sailed south from Panama in 1522 in search of a rumored destination, "Pirú"—the name was really that of a mythical chieftain but would later be transformed into Peru and identified with an empire. There was more than just a chieftain to be found, but it took a decade of coastal reconnaissance and humiliating failure before Pizarro, his brothers, and their partner Diego de Almagro, marched at last into the Inca Empire (see fig. 4). In the meantime Pizarro had acquired Quechua translators steeped for several years in Castilian Spanish, a small army of men with horses, armor, and state-of-the-art weapons, and also a license to invade from Charles V.

Tawantinsuyu, the Inca world, was in a succession crisis in 1532. In the five years since the death of the Inca Huayna Capac, two of his sons, Atahualpa and Huascar, had battled for control. When Pizarro and his 168 men climbed into the northern Andes to meet the emperor in the sacred city of Cajamarca, Atahualpa was flush with a recent victory over his brother. Far from apprehensive, Atahualpa intended, rather like Moctezuma in Mexico, to draft the strangely bearded and well-armed foreigners into his service. Though their horses, firearms, and steel swords were cause for wonder, the Spanish were not mistaken for gods. Andeans and Mesoamericans alike saw the Spaniards and their African slaves as foreign men to be examined and turned away, accommodated, or used, as circumstances allowed.

Conquistador custom, however, was to initiate a diplomatic encounter that would then treacherously turn into a violent taking of hostages—preferably the seizure of the king. In November 1532, in a surprise attack at a diplomatic meeting, Pizarro and his men captured Atahualpa. Having supplied the foreigners with food and lodging, Atahualpa had no reason to suspect that they would seek to kidnap and ransom, much less murder him. Humiliated, Atahualpa was held hostage for nearly a year as his subjects scrambled to gather up gold and silver to free him. The Inca possessed far more gold and silver than the Aztecs, and the hoard of metals offered to free their leader, whom most Andeans regarded as a divine being, was staggering. Suddenly Pizarro and his followers were rich beyond their wildest dreams. The word "Peru" thus became instantly synonymous with great wealth among Europeans, an association that would soon be reinforced with the discovery of immensely rich silver mines. Despite the ransom, however, the Inca Atahualpa was executed in 1533 on Pizarro's orders. The treachery was complete. And yet the true military conquest of Tawantinsuyu was yet to come.

The first military stage of the Spanish conquest of the Inca Empire continued through the 1530s. As in Mexico, the fighting was the work of a confederation of indigenous peoples who resented Inca supremacy and who accepted the Spaniards as arbitrators uncompromised by immersion in native politics. First Cuzco, then Quito, the empire's two capitals, were captured in 1534. But there remained an incumbent Inca, Manco Capac. Spaniards later portrayed Manco as a puppet of the Pizarro regime, an heir to Atahualpa's throne only by the grace of the Spaniards. But in Andean eyes, Manco was the legitimate ruler; in the account of the conquest by his son and subsequent Inca ruler, Titu Cusi Yupanqui, Manco had been the legitimate emperor since before the Spaniards had appeared. From the perspective of Manco and those loyal to him, Atahualpa and Huascar had been mere usurpers; their deaths did not mark the conquest of the Inca Empire but rather its return to legitimate rule.

Abused by the Spaniards, who repeatedly demanded not only large payments of gold and silver from Manco but also the most beautiful of his wives, Manco attempted to expel the rude invaders from Cuzco in 1536. He almost succeeded. Forced to retreat down the Urubamba River, past Pachacuti's palace complex at Machu Picchu, Manco established a rump Inca state in the wet lowlands, at a site called Vilcabamba. There he and a

4. Francisco Pizarro and Diego de Almagro. Two images from a unique
account of conquest-era Andean history, the 1615 *Nueva corónica y buen
gobierno* by Felipe Guaman Poma de Ayala, a mestizo of mixed Spanish
and native Andean ancestry. On this page Diego de Almagro and Francisco
Pizarro, the original partners in the first invasion of the Inca Empire.
Opposite, a decade later in Spanish Peru, Almagro's mestizo son assassinates
Pizarro.

CONQVISTA
A DŌ FRAN⁰ PIŠARO LE MA

TO EL DŌ DI. DE AL MAGRO

el mesmo capitan y conquistador fuesu
padre don diego dealmagro el biejo

almagro

pisaro

enlima

series of successors, including his son Titu Cusi, maintained the Inca "empire" until 1572.

Meanwhile, with so much wealth and territory at stake, Spanish conquistadors began battling one another, and eventually the Crown, for control of Peru. There were violent disagreements between the followers of Pizarro and those of Diego de Almagro, Francisco Pizarro's original partner. After several attempted compromises, Pizarro had Almagro executed as a rebel, only to be murdered in turn by his former ally's son in 1541 (see fig. 4). There were other contenders for Peru as well, such as Pedro de Alvarado, fresh from his putative conquest of Guatemala. Despite command of a large and well-equipped expedition, Alvarado lost his way in the jungles of coastal Ecuador and arrived in Quito too late to share in the plunder. Sebastián de Benalcázar, one of Pizarro's captains, had beat him there in a highland march from the south. Benalcázar would continue north beyond Cali, in what is now Colombia, where he met still other conquistadors heading south from the Caribbean coast in search of a mythical chieftain the Spanish called El Dorado.

As the Spanish invasion of native lands pushed farther and farther from the old imperial centers, representatives of Charles V intervened in hopes of establishing order and collecting taxes in precious metals. Among the new proclamations was one limiting conquistador access to *encomiendas* (the grants of native labor and tribute given to encomenderos). Another was a law that banned the enslavement of native peoples in the Americas. Las Casas's arguments at court had won the day, but there was little the friar could do to ensure that the so-called New Laws were enforced. In Peru, conquistador outrage sparked a revolt and civil war that lasted until 1548. In the end, the Crown prevailed but not before a viceroy was killed in battle and Gonzalo Pizarro, another of Francisco Pizarro's younger brothers, was captured and executed as a rebel. The laws were soon whittled down by compromises, while unhappy conquistadors continued to rebel against Crown authority until the 1570s.

"Compass and sword augment the score, more and more and more and more"

Not all expeditions fit neatly into the schema of the two chains; the most obvious exception is that of the Jiménez de Quesada campaign into Colombia, which came directly from the Canary Islands. But by and large the expeditions that bypassed the chain were later attempts to conquer and settle regions that had been ignored for one reason or another—or they were vain misguided quests for promised lands or rich native realms that did not exist. An example is the disastrous 1550s campaign led directly from Seville by don Pedro de Mendoza down the Río de la Plata. The river's name was a symbol of the wishful thinking that underlay the expedition (*plata* means silver). Mendoza had hoped for another Peru but found nothing even close to it; within a few months, two-thirds of the 1,500 Spaniards had died, mostly from starvation.

During the second half of the sixteenth century, Mexico and Peru were consolidated as unchallenged colonial centers. Where native empires had dominated in the previous century, Spanish-native kingdoms now radiated power and wealth, funding the continual pushing back of the conquest frontier. Yet by century's end there were still conquistadors fighting in numerous corners of the Americas. The inscription on the frontispiece of Vargas Machuca's *Indian Militia* of 1599—"Compass and sword augment the score, More and more and more and more" (see fig. 8 in chap. 5)—was less a reference to past conquests than a continued call to arms, a rallying cry to keep up the conquistador spirit.

Was the bloody, long-drawn nature of the conquest of the Maya more a tribute to Spanish conquistador spirit or the Maya tradition of dogged resistance? It is hard to say. Archaeologists once spoke of Maya empires, but that was before the hieroglyphs were deciphered. It is now abundantly clear that, for millennia, Maya city-states tried in vain to dominate their neighbors, developing ideologies of divine kingship that might have underpinned empires as impressive as the Aztec and Inca. Yet the losers in such wars refused to be subdued by their neighbors, let alone by outsiders. In the sixteenth and seventeenth centuries, they similarly resisted Spanish and Nahua invaders. Colonies were established in Maya country but only after years of punishing warfare—and only in pockets of the Maya area.

Although Spaniards had suffered bruising encounters with Maya warriors along the Yucatec coast in the 1510s, the assault on the Maya first began in earnest in 1524–29. That half-decade saw two massive invasions of the Guatemalan highlands, led first by Pedro de Alvarado (see fig. 6 in chap. 3) and then by his brother Jorge. The Alvarados seemed to have two major advantages. First, the highlands were dominated by two rival kingdoms, those of the Kaqchikel and K'iche' Maya; their enmity could be exploited, setting one against the other and using both to pick off the smaller kingdoms and city-states that surrounded them. This was the predictable Spanish strategy, but it collapsed under the weight of Pedro's heavy-handedness and Maya intransigence. The second advantage was the size of the invading force—not the Spaniards per se, who numbered a few hundred, but their allies. Pedro brought some six thousand Aztecs, Tlaxcalans, Zapotecs, Mixtecs, and other Mesoamericans. Jorge's allied force was even larger, comprising up to ten thousand Aztecs and other central Mexican warriors. The impact of such a force was devastating, and the highlands were virtually destroyed in order for them to be conquered. In the end, it was the indigenous conquistadors who made a colony in the highlands possible. The survivors stayed as settlers, contributing to the creation of colonial Guatemala.

Meanwhile, a similar tale unfolded to the north, in Yucatan. There Spaniards led by Francisco de Montejo failed to encounter either an empire to topple or a source of great wealth. As in Guatemala, a handful of kingdoms with a history of conflict seemed ripe for a divide-and-conquer strategy. But Maya rulers proved as adept as using the Spanish invaders as the Spaniards did at manipulating them. Beginning in 1527, it took the Montejos (father, son, and nephew) three invasions and two decades to secure a colony in the north. As in the Guatemalan highlands, victory came only after the importation of thousands of allied central Mexican warriors, and after the majority of the Maya populations had succumbed to disease and violence.

Still, the Spanish colonies of Yucatan and Guatemala in the late sixteenth century excluded most of the Maya area. Spanish maps marked the miles between the two colonies as *despoblado* ("uninhabited"), but that fiction masked the failure of colonial authorities to conquer all the Maya. The border periodically expanded, but at times it also contracted. The Spanish town of Bacalar, located in the middle of the Maya area near the Caribbean coast, was abandoned in the 1630s for a century. The colonial border at the southwest base of the peninsula shifted dramatically in the 1660s with a Maya "rebellion," as Spanish officials called the migration of thousands of Maya out of the drought-ridden colony into independent kingdoms of the so-called despoblado. The largest such kingdom, that of the Itzá Maya, actually grew in the seventeenth century, until its bloody and expensive destruction in 1697 by an invasion force of Spaniards, free-colored militiamen, and Maya from Yucatan.

One factor in the destruction of the Itzá kingdom was the role played by Ah Chan, a nephew of the Itzá king. In 1695 Ah Chan had been sent to Mérida, the capital of the colony in Yucatan, as an ambassador of peace and submission. The king hoped that a nominal recognition of colonial control might save his seat on the throne. Ah Chan converted to Christianity and was baptized Martín Chan, after his new godfather, don Martín de Ursúa, the governor of Yucatan and soon-to-be conqueror of the Itzás. Ah Chan remained loyal to this strategy of appeasement through the Spanish invasion of the Itzá kingdom, only abandoning the Spaniards six months after the kingdom's conquest. Concluding, with good reason, that Spanish colonial rule was a disaster in the region, he became a leader of the Itzá resistance, ruling an independent kingdom of Itzá, Chol, and Mopan Maya in the forests of what is now northern Guatemala and Belize until at least 1757.

The Maya area was not the only part of the Americas where Spanish conquistador activities lacked either the dramatic narrative of the invasions of the Aztecs and Inca, or the swift, tragic conclusions of campaigns like Mendoza's down the Rio de la Plata. In the Chocó region of today's Colombia, the Citará and their neighbors endured decimation by disease, harrowing warfare, enslavement, and forced relocation by missionaries. As with the Maya area, it is hard to say which phenomenon exhibits greater tenacity, the onslaught of conquistador and colonists or indigenous refusal to submit. Both Spaniards and natives seemed trapped in conflict for centuries. The "conquest" or violent "pacification" of the Chocó lasted for most of the three centuries of the colonial period. People simply refused to be moved, put to work, or change how they married and buried their dead. In the 1680s natives whom Spaniards called "rebels" killed 126 Spaniards and their African slaves, and drove out the rest. The empire fought back, and eventually some natives were converted. Spanish culture had a long-term impact in other ways, as local people adopted new material goods and farm animals, and learned to use the Spanish legal system to defend themselves.

New Mexico had a similar history: a colony, incorporated into the monarchy with dazzling ambition and heartbreaking hardship in 1598, vanished in a ferocious native insurrection in 1680, only to be systematically and bloodily forced back into allegiance and thinly resettled by missionaries and frontiersmen. The cost of that second conquest was one that could never be recouped.

The indigenous people with the most persistent and astonishing record of resistance to the conquistadors (and to all foreign invaders) are the Mapuche. The homeland of the Mapuche or Araucanians (a term derived from the Arauca River) is the rugged coastline, gently rolling hills, and dense temperate rainforests at the foot of South America. Spanish conquistadors found that peoples recently conquered by native empires—such as the Nahuas, Mixtecs, and other subjects of the Aztec Empire—were relatively easily drawn into the new colony. By the same token, those who had a tradition of resisting imperial encroachment were often the hardest to conquer. The Mapuche were such a people; they had resisted the Inca for a century, and went on to resist the colonial Spanish and the Chilean nation-state for another four centuries. Their success was partly cultural; boys were reared for a life of warfare, and military prowess was prized above other virtues. But the Mapuche were also able to appropriate two well-tried conquistador advantages: they quickly adopted horses, guns, knives, and steel swords; and they stymied attempts at divide-and-conquer strategies by forging long-term confederations with indigenous neighbors.

Spain never conquered the Mapuche. Not until the 1880s did Chilean armed forces manage to partially subdue them using modern weapons, forced deportation, and threats of genocide—a process similar to that used against native peoples of the plains of Argentina and of the North American West in the same era.

Chapter 3
To give account of who I am

"I speak about that which concerns myself and all the true conquerors, my companions, who served His Majesty by discovering, conquering, pacifying, and settling most of the provinces," wrote veteran conquistador Bernal Díaz del Castillo to the Spanish king. His purpose, he stated, was "to give account of who I am so that Your Majesty may deign to do me fuller favors." Like many of his compatriots, Díaz felt obliged to repeatedly "give account" of who he was because the "favors" granted to him never matched up to his sacrifices and achievements. By the time he died in 1585, after seventy years in the New World, he was but one of thousands of conquistador-settlers who had struggled to gain royal recognition. Those men watched a small minority acquire great fortunes, considerable status, and, for a few, lasting fame. Two became legends. Ironically, it was men like Bernal Díaz who contributed to the formation of those legends.

Cortés and Pizarro, as the "great captains" who led the invasions of the two Native American empires, achieved a renown in their lifetimes that has survived, even grown, to this day. A recent history of the Spanish Empire described Cortés and Pizarro as the Emperor Charles V's "two most important subjects," and the three of them together as "the three greatest men of the age." That claim aside, there is no doubt that if we begin our own account of who the conquistadors were by starting at the apex of the pyramid of renown and working down, we must begin with Cortés and Pizarro.

After those two, who are the next three who achieved lasting fame? The exercise is not trivial, for the conquistadors themselves argued at length over who were the greatest to follow in the footsteps of the conquerors of the Aztecs and Inca. Jiménez de Quesada, for example, wrote to the king in 1576 that he was considered the third most important captain in conquest history (but, he claimed, some ranked him first in terms of the quality and lucre of his conquests). Based on the amount of space devoted to specific conquistadors in his *Indian Militia*, Vargas Machuca ranked Jiménez de Quesada second, between Cortés and Pizarro—with no other conquistadors receiving more than passing mention.

With apologies to Jiménez de Quesada, we have selected—in addition to Cortés and Pizarro—three others to round out a top five: Pedro de Alvarado, Francisco de Montejo (the elder), and Hernando de Soto. Based on Internet hits at the time of writing, conquistador name recognition in the modern world ranks Juan Ponce de León, Álvar Núñez Cabeza de Vaca, Francisco Vásquez de Coronado, and Hernando de Soto (in that order) ahead of the likes of Cortés, Pizarro, Alvarado, and Montejo. This is probably because they all played the most prominent roles in the early exploration of territories that would eventually become part of the United States (and the Internet is skewed toward the English-speaking world). Of those four, we selected Soto simply because the geographical scope of his conquest experiences makes him arguably more representative of conquistadors in general (although Cabeza de Vaca might have served equally well).

Hernando Cortés was born in the early 1480s in Medellín, Extremadura, a dry, poor region of western Spain. He was the son of an illegitimate lesser nobleman, Martín Cortés. As a young man he probably began—at least—a course in law at the university in Salamanca. But he found sedentary life dull or unremunerative and went to Valencia with the intention of seeking his fortune with the Spanish forces fighting in Italy. That ambition—to achieve glory and status through military accomplishment in the Mediterranean—never left him; even after his war against the Aztecs he aspired to fight in Italy, Africa, and the Holy Land. But in his early twenties he was led elsewhere, to the Caribbean, where many real and fictional pícaros, outcasts, and social or financial failures would seek their fortunes, unrestrained by the restricted acceptance back home. There he spent more than a dozen years as a conquistador-settler on Hispaniola and Cuba, followed by a decade of exploration and conquest in Mesoamerica.

Cortés then returned to Spain, and in 1529, shortly after meeting with the king in Toledo, he encountered Francisco Pizarro, who was there seeking a royal license to invade Peru. Cortés's mother was a Pizarro, and he was therefore a distant relation of the Pizarro brothers—Francisco, Gonzalo, Hernando, and Juan, all of whom participated in the Spanish invasion of the Inca Empire. Like Cortés, the Pizarros were from Extremadura—from the town of Trujillo. Their father was a lesser nobleman and a veteran of the wars in Italy. Francisco was an illegitimate son by a local farmer's daughter. Francisco was never legitimated; he remained all his life illiterate, a consummate gambler, and a man more at home fighting or working with his hands than governing or discussing matters of law (in this respect he was very different from Cortés, whose letters to the king are artfully composed).

Pizarro briefly visited Italy. Like Cortés, he came close to pursuing a career there. But he too chose "the Indies" over Italy—and sailed with an uncle to the Caribbean. Just as Cortés won encomiendas in Cuba, so did Pizarro win them in Panama. It is not clear how close Francisco was to his brothers in childhood, but they were ready to follow him after 1529—including Hernando, the eldest and only legitimate brother. In that year, Francisco added to his two and a half decades of conquest experience in the Americas a royal license to invade Peru.

Conquest campaigns were family affairs; just as Pizarro pursued ambition in the Americas with his brothers, so did Pedro de Alvarado. Likewise a native of Extremadura (from the town of Badajoz), Alvarado arrived in Hispaniola in 1510 with his five brothers and one of their uncles; he would later invade Guatemala with three of his brothers and three cousins. Pedro participated in the Conquest of Cuba and was a member of the 1518 expedition of exploration along the coast of Yucatan and Mexico. He played a major role in the Cortés-led war against the Aztecs; had Cortés been killed during that war, Alvarado most likely would have taken command of the campaign, as he was left in charge of Spanish and Tlaxcalan forces in Tenochtitlán in 1520, while Cortés was temporarily out of the city. His reputation as a hothead originated in his impulsive leadership during those weeks. By attacking the Aztecs during a religious festival, he broke the stand-off and forced the Spanish-Tlaxcalan force onto the defensive; the result was the Noche Triste, the death of hundreds of Spaniards and thousands of Tlaxcalans during their escape from the city.

Alvarado's blond hair, as well as his infamous temper, earned him the Nahuatl nickname *Tonatiuh* ("Sun"; see fig. 6). The violence of his 1524–26 invasion of highland Guatemala consolidated that reputation. Wounded and disillusioned, Pedro left his brother Jorge to re-invade Guatemala in the late 1520s. Although it was Jorge and his tens of thousands of Nahua allies who finally crushed Maya resistance sufficiently to establish a colony in the highlands, it was Pedro who was granted the governorship. But like Cortés and most other conquistadors, Alvarado viewed every conquest campaign as another link in a chain of conquests. In 1534, hearing news of the Inca Empire, he exploited Guatemalan resources to lead an expedition to Peru. Bought out by rival Spaniards who had arrived before him, he turned his attentions to Honduras; he was governor of a small, half-hearted Spanish colony there until being edged out by Francisco de Montejo in 1540. Ever restive, the following year he led a campaign to put down the Mixton Revolt, a native rebellion in Nueva Galicia (north of Mexico). It would prove to be his final campaign.

Whereas Pizarro and Alvarado brought along and fought alongside their brothers, the three Francisco de Montejos who campaigned in the Americas were father, son, and nephew (see fig. 5). Natives of Salamanca, they participated variously in the protracted conquest of Yucatan, although it was the elder Montejo who held the adelantado license. In the late 1510s (Montejo was then about thirty-five years old) he crossed to Cuba, then to Mexico with Cortés, before returning to Spain to secure that license. Acquiring it in 1526, he then spent a decade attempting to establish colonies in Tabasco, Yucatan, and Honduras, with little success. When he was finally able to administer colonies as governor, it was as much or more due to the efforts of others: in Honduras, starting in 1540, thanks partly to Alvarado; and in Yucatan, starting in 1546, thanks to the invasion campaign into the peninsula led by his son and nephew.

Like so many conquistadors, therefore, Montejo the elder spent years of frustrating campaigning, both militarily and politically— he spent more time in Spain seeking a license to conquer Yucatan than he did governing a colony there, and even more on failed invasions. Like Jiménez de Quesada, for every month of relished success Montejo endured years battling lawyers and courtiers, tropical discomforts and indigenous hostiles. Montejo's reliance on others—family members, partners, conquistador rivals, not to mention native allies—also made his experience typical.

Hernando de Soto left Spain to seek advancement in the Indies when Montejo did (in 1514) but at a more typical age for a fledgling conqueror (Soto was about twenty). His career of almost thirty years of exploration and fighting in the Americas comprised three stages. For most of his career, he participated in conquest

5. The façade of the Montejo Palace. Conquistadors often sought to memorialize their accomplishments in imagery inscribed on coats of arms, painted into portraits, or cut in stone on public façades. One of the best-known examples is that of the two Franciscos de Montejo, father and son. Their likenesses were carved on the portal of the palatial Montejo residence on the central plaza of Mérida, the capital city of the new colony of Yucatan, built in the 1540s. The conquistador pair are depicted standing on open-mouthed severed heads; it is not clear if they are the heads of conquered Maya warriors, of generic barbarians, or the heads of defeated Spanish rivals. On either side are sculptures of the mythical "wild men" of medieval Europe, symbolizing the barbarity supposedly crushed by the civilizing impact of the Montejo triumph.

campaigns and settlement efforts in Central America, ending up as an encomendero in Nicaragua. There he may have languished, having missed out on the great opportunity of these years—the Conquest of Mexico—were it not for word of the Pizarro-Almagro expedition to Peru. He joined that expedition in time (1532) and brought enough men with him to be made a captain and participate in the great division of spoils resulting from the captures of Atahualpa and the Inca cities of Cajamarca and Cuzco. He then left in time (1534) to avoid a violent death in the conquest campaigns and civil wars that marked Peru's history for the next decade or so.

Soto returned to Spain, transformed from a relatively obscure conqueror-settler in Central America to a celebrated and wealthy conquistador of Peru; he made a highly advantageous marriage, was admitted into the Order of Santiago, and was appointed governor of Cuba, with an adelantado license for Florida. He might have rested on his laurels in Havana. But instead, in 1539, he embarked on the third and final stage of his career, leading into North America the massive expedition of exploration that would leave his wife a widow, besmirch his reputation in the Spanish world but eventually earn him lasting fame.

Soto died from an unknown illness, on today's Louisiana-Arkansas border. One way or another, most conquistadors died in the field. For example, all but one of the Pizarro brothers died violent deaths—Francisco was assassinated by the son of his partner (Diego de Almagro; see fig. 4), Juan died during Manco's siege of Cuzco, and Gonzalo was executed as a traitor. Only Hernando passed away peacefully, dying a blind old man, in 1578, on the vast family estates outside Trujillo (Spain) acquired with wealth taken from Peru. Pedro de Alvarado, meanwhile, perished in 1541, crushed by his own horse as it lost its footing during a retreat from an attack on native rebels (see fig. 6).

As for Cortés and his ambition to be governor, perhaps viceroy, of New Spain: upon his return to Spain, he was well received by Charles V, but the king was wisely reluctant to make conquistadors into viceroys. Cortés was therefore bought off with a title and enormous encomienda holdings in Mexico (he became the marquis of the Valley of Oaxaca). In 1547, after participating in a failed expedition to North Africa, Cortés died in Seville. Shortly after, in 1550, his old conquest colleague Francisco de Montejo also returned to Spain—recalled to defend his performance as Yucatan's first governor—where he died within a few years.

6. The death of Pedro de Alvarado, as depicted by a native artist in the Codex Telleriano-Remensis. Alvarado died violently, as most conquistadors did. In addition to the Spanish gloss, a sun glyph identifies him by his Nahuatl nickname, Tonatiuh ("Sun"). Painted by Nahua artists in Mexico in the 1550s, the codex gives Alvarado two features typical of native depictions of Spanish conquistadors—both of them more accurate than many Spanish renderings, especially later ones. One is the bushy beard; the Spanish ability to grow a full beard was noteworthy to native observers, and the difficulties of shaving during conquest campaigns meant that conquistadors tended to sport beards, despite their being unfashionable in Europe at the time. The other feature is his clothing; Alvarado is wearing a sixteenth-century skirted doublet, not the full armor that Spanish painters tended to give the conquerors.

Marauding wolves

How typical were the famous five conquistadors just described? In the obvious sense of their fame, they were not typical at all. The vast majority of the conquistadors died in obscurity. Furthermore, the identities, experiences, and life stories of the Spaniards who participated in the conquests in the Americas were varied.

Yet in many ways the five were no different from all the other "tyrannical captains"—as Las Casas labeled them. In the Dominican friar's hyperbolic depiction, the conquistadors were all wolves preying on indigenous sheep. Whether "great tyrants" (as Las Casas called Alvarado and Pizarro), "wretched men" (Montejo), or any of the other "bad" and "cruel" Spaniards who followed them, they all responded to the presence of the "gentle lambs and sheep" by becoming "like fierce wolves and tigers and lions." Or as Michael de Carvajal put it in his 1557 play, *Complaint of the Indians in the Court of Death*, "these thieving" or "marauding wolves" (*estos lobos robadores*); "these human beasts of prey" (*estas gentes y rapinas*).

We might have included a sixth famous conquistador—or rather, infamous anti-heroic conquistador—as an extreme example of the "marauding wolf": Lope de Aguirre. The son of a Basque nobleman, inspired by tales of the discovery of the Inca Empire to travel to Peru in his twenties, Aguirre's life as a conquistador began in fairly typical fashion. "I crossed the sea to the land of Peru," he later wrote to the king, "to win fame with lance in hand, and to meet the obligations of all good men." From the late 1530s to the late 1550s, Aguirre participated in conquest activities from Nicaragua to Bolivia, as well as fighting in the civil war that Spaniards waged in Peru in the 1540s. But along the way, he acquired a reputation as a man of particular cruelty, a torturer and murderer.

This was something of an achievement in the context of the conquest world—a world in which Pedro de Alvarado committed widely known atrocities with impunity, in which Jiménez de Quesada's violence seems nothing out of the ordinary, in which Las Casas detailed the brutality of one "tyrannical captain" after another. Wars nurture sociopaths, and if we are looking for examples in the sixteenth century, Aguirre is the place to start. His swan song was to turn a 1560 expedition down the Amazon River into an orgy of violence, culminating in his takeover of the Spanish colony on Margarita Island, where he slaughtered most of the local officials and settlers. Claiming that "they tried to kill me," he explained that "I hung them all." Captured in Barquisimeto in 1561, he was executed as a traitor and the pieces of his dismembered body distributed around the colony of Venezuela.

It is easy to dismiss Aguirre as too extreme a case to be illustrative. Certainly almost all his actions in his final year—from murdering his own daughter to writing to the king to justify his treason and signing the letter, "I, rebel until death against you for your ingratitude"—seem to underscore his nickname of *El Loco*, the madman. Yet he was an extreme example along the same spectrum of origins, experiences, and actions as the other conquistadors. Aguirre was hardly the only conquistador to earn a nasty reputation. Nuño de Guzmán was denounced by Las Casas as "the most despicable and evil" of New Spain's conquistadors, and modern historians described him as "a natural gangster" (J. H. Parry), "ambitious, ruthless" (Ida Altman), "the personification of the Black Legend" (Donald Chipman). Yet—as governor of a Mexican province and first president of New Spain's *audiencia* or high court—he enjoyed offices way beyond Aguirre's grasp. Nor was Aguirre the only Spaniard to butcher native peoples, murder rival compatriots, rebel against the Crown, fail to navigate well the political world of early colonial Spanish America, and die an ignominious death.

Even Aguirre's seemingly crazy last letter to the king contains much of the characteristics of a typical probanza report. It contains almost formulaic language about service and sacrifice, about "conquering Indians and founding towns," about "answering the call" of the king to defend his dominions against rebels and the true faith against Lutherans. Aguirre's crossing of the line to insult the king and declare himself in revolt is shocking because it is rare—it is deranged because it defeats the entire purpose of the genre. But the brief autobiography of service, the ranting against bad local officials, the harping on war wounds, the undertone of bitterness, all are standard conventions of conquistador rhetoric.

Rhetoric and (in)famous cases aside, then, it is clear that the conquistadors came from similar backgrounds and had similar goals in the Americas—where they responded to the conditions of conquest in similar ways and enjoyed or suffered similar careers. The patterns of conquistador biographies thus reveal a set of representative characteristics. From these we can construct a conquistador type, one who echoes in some respects the tiny minority whose names became legend.

That type was a young man in his late-twenties, semiliterate, from southwestern Spain, trained in a particular trade or profession, seeking opportunity through patronage networks based on family and hometown ties. Armed as well as he could afford, and with some experience already of exploration and conquest in the Americas, he would be ready to invest what he had and risk his life—if absolutely necessary—in order to be a member of the first company to conquer somewhere wealthy and well populated.

Our conquistador type was not a soldier in the armies of the king of Spain. Although the conquistadors are often misleadingly referred to as soldiers—and they were certainly armed, organized, and experienced in military matters—they acquired their martial skills from conflict situations in the Americas, not from formal training. Expedition members tended to be recruited in recently founded colonies; the New World inexperience of Jiménez de Quesada and others brought from the Canaries in 1536 was atypical, as most participants in conquest expeditions already had some experience in the Americas. Among the Spaniards who participated in the famous capture of Atahualpa at Cajamarca, at least two-thirds had prior conquest experience and more than half had spent at least five years in the Americas. But none of this amounted to formal training.

This lack of formal training was paralleled by a lack of formal ranking; Spanish forces in Europe at this time were led by commanders from the high nobility and organized into various ranks. In contrast, conquistador groups were headed by captains, the sole named rank and one that varied in number. The record of the division of spoils at Cajamarca listed the men in two categories only, *gente de a caballo* (men on horseback) and *gente de a pie* (men on foot). A man could move from one category to the other by buying a horse (or losing one).

Because conquistadors were not soldiers in a formal army, their dress, armor, and weaponry were individualized. Lacking an official uniform, each company member dressed according to his occupation, status, and wealth—with adjustments made during the course of an expedition. But there was a basic dress common to all Spaniards, consisting of leggings, a pullover tunic, and an unadorned cloak. The better-off wore an outer garment such as a doublet or jerkin, trimmed with silk or fur if possible (see fig. 6). These typically had buttons from the neck down, with fitted waists and small skirts; styles varied, and evolved, during the sixteenth century (the doublet eventually became the modern jacket). Spaniards rapidly replaced or altered European dress during conquest campaigns, out of two different necessities: clothing from Spain was scare and expensive; and American climates required adaptation for survival's sake. Wool, flax, and linen gave way to cotton; heavy doublets gave way to the *xicolli* and the *tilmatli*, the short jacket and rectangular cape worn by Aztecs and other Central Mexicans (or the cotton ponchos of the Andeans); shoes and boots gave way to sandals.

The conquest paintings and screens that were popular in seventeenth-century Mexico often depict entire conquistador companies in full body armor and helmets. But such paintings are laden with anachronisms and imagined details, the inclusion of armor being one of them. Earlier drawings and textual evidence suggests that Spaniards seldom wore armor, that such armor was primarily limited to iron breastplates, and those were carried with the supplies to be put on only at the onset of battle. From the 1520s on, Spaniards in Mesoamerica adopted the *ichcahuipilli*

of the Aztecs. This quilted cotton vest was designed to protect the
torso from the obsidian weapons used by native Mesoamericans,
and it was more appropriate to the American climate and more
readily available than iron armor. Round, iron shields were
brought from Spain but were less common than wooden and
leather ones, which could be more easily made in the Americas
or replaced by native shields. Likewise, iron helmets were less
common than flat caps, skullcaps, and simple war hats. The
elegant, crested helmet called the *morion*, typically shown on the
head of Cortés and other conquerors in later paintings, did not
become common in Europe until the 1540s and was never worn
by conquistadors.

The typical conquistador carried a broadsword. Although Toledo
swordsmiths perfected rapiers and other lighter, slimmer,
sharper—but equally strong—weapons in the sixteenth century,
the Spaniards who fought native warriors in the 1520s and
1530s typically wielded blunt-tipped three-footers. Some
carried broadswords five or six feet long, which were swung
with two hands and could devastate massed native warriors.
Spanish accounts frequently describe long battles in which
native forces suffer high casualties while inflicting only wounds
on the invaders. Issues of exaggeration aside, such outcomes
were possible because of the disparities in length and durability
between Spanish steel swords and native weapons made of wood
and obsidian.

A less prestigious, less important—but still significant—weapon
carried by some conquistadors was the twelve-foot lance. These
could also be used as pikes and could be made in the field, using
recycled iron tips, and there is evidence that the allied native
warriors that accompanied Spaniards on almost every expedition
soon learned to make and use these lances. Still, they were less
useful than in Europe, because native enemies had no cavalry.
Similarly, the European crossbow was often highly effective and
relatively easy to repair in the Americas. But its use was restricted

to small units of bowmen, who tended to be outnumbered many times over by skilled archers among the native allies.

Did the typical conquistador carry a gun? Probably not. The matchlock first appeared in the Americas within a few years of Columbus's first voyage across the Atlantic, barely a decade after its invention, and colonial-period accounts make much of its impact on native warriors. But the matchlock of the conquistador era was a clumsy, unreliable weapon, ill-suited to the tropics. Mostly known as the harquebus—*arcabuz* or *escopeta* in Spanish— this long-barreled gun required dry powder, often misfired, and took longer to reload than an Aztec, Maya, or Inca archer took to unleash dozens of arrows. Again, later paintings are misleading, as they sometimes show conquistadors with muskets—a more useful matchlock handgun that was not invented until the 1550s. The harquebus's greatest virtue in the conquest wars was its psychological impact, a display weapon that could be deployed selectively to impress and terrify the enemy.

This was also true—but on a larger, more dramatic scale—of the cannon. Even small cannon made a deafening sound, spat fire, and could throw a ball some 2,000 yards; Spaniards claimed that natives were petrified by the cannon's apparent ability to harness the power of thunder and lightning. But, like the matchlock, their utility in combat was highly limited. Take, for example, Cortés's deployment of cannon on his invasion of the Aztec Empire in 1519–21. He landed on the Mexican coast with ten brass lombards, but they were too heavy to move inland. He was able to move the smaller (three-inch-bore) falconets, but he only had four of them. They could be used only in dry weather and with enough warning to mount them on makeshift carriages. Furthermore, they were all lost in the lake surrounding the Aztec capital of Tenochtitlán when the Spaniards and their allies were forced to flee the city at night (the so-called *Noche Triste*). Only with considerable planning, effort, time, and native assistance was Cortés able to transport the lombards into the Valley of Mexico to use in the 1521 siege of Tenochtitlán.

Why did the typical conquistador cross the Atlantic, or, once settled in the Americas, join a company to further risk his life? Simply put, conquistadors were motivated by a search for economic and social opportunity. The letters Cortés wrote to the king, published in the conquistador's lifetime and still in print today in many languages, give the impression that Spaniards were driven by a sense of loyalty to Crown and church. This image of the conquistadors was constructed for the benefit of the king, who was well aware of the personal ambitions and motives of the conquerors.

But nor should Spaniards be seen as gold-thirsty, despite the common depiction of the conquistadors as crazed by an "epidemic of gold" (*pestilencia de oro*; Carvajal's phrase). Conquistadors sought gold and silver for fundamentally practical reasons: precious metals were the only nonperishable easy-to-ship item of value that could pay the merchants and creditors who funded conquest campaigns. Conquistadors "were neither paid nor forced but went of their own will and at their own cost," in the words of one of them, Francisco de Jérez.

Gaspar de Marquina, like Jérez, followed Pizarro into the Inca Empire. Marquina wrote to his father that he went to Peru because it was a place where "there's more gold and silver than iron in Biscay, and more sheep than in Soria, and great supplies of all kinds of food, and much fine clothing, and the best people that have been seen in the whole Indies, and many great lords among them." Marquina was not a professional soldier but a page, a fully literate, high-ranking servant to two of the early conquistador-governors of Spanish American colonies, Governor Pedrarias Dávila of Nicaragua and Francisco Pizarro. He came to "the Indies" of his own free will, hoping to return to his father in Spain a wealthy man and, most likely, take up a career as a notary or merchant. He pursued that opportunity through his connection to important patrons. However, like most Spaniards who fought in the violent invasions of the early sixteenth century, he died before he could return to Spain—in Marquina's case, killed in a skirmish with native Andeans by the time his father had received his letter and the gold bar accompanying it.

Spaniards, then, joined conquest expeditions not in return for specified payments but in the hope of acquiring wealth and status. Spaniards called these ventures "companies." While powerful patrons played important investment roles, it was the captains who primarily funded companies and expected to reap the greatest rewards. The spirit of commercialism infused conquest expeditions from start to finish, with participants selling services and trading goods with each other throughout the endeavor. The conquerors were, in other words, armed entrepreneurs. The members of a successful conquest company hoped to be granted an encomienda, as its access to indigenous labor and tribute afforded a conquistador high status and often a superior lifestyle among fellow colonists. As there were never enough encomiendas to go around, the most lucrative grants went to those who had invested the most in the expedition—and survived to see it succeed. Lesser investors received lesser grants—a few dozen, instead of thousands, of indigenous "vassals"—or simply a share of the spoils of war.

Conquistadors were overwhelmingly middle-ranking men, from occupations and backgrounds below the high nobility but above the commoner masses. In the wake of the founding of the city of Panama in 1519, the ninety-eight Spanish conquistador-settlers were asked to identify themselves and their professions. Seventy-five responded. Only two of them claimed to be professional soldiers. Sixty percent claimed to be professional men and artisans, occupations from the middle ranks of society. A similar analysis of the conquerors of the New Kingdom of Granada (today's Colombia) is less precise as to occupations and probably exaggerates the numbers of middle-ranking men. Nevertheless, the data clearly shows that men of some means or property, professionals, and entrepreneurs of some kind predominated.

Likewise, those Spaniards at Cajamarca in 1533 who recorded their occupations were not career soldiers but professionals and artisans who had acquired various battle experience and martial skills. A third of those who stated their occupation were artisans—including tailors, horseshoers, carpenters, trumpeters, a cooper, a swordsmith, a stonemason, a barber, and a piper/crier. The same kinds of artisans had also accompanied Francisco de Montejo on his first expedition into Yucatan in 1527, along with the usual professional men—merchants, physicians, a couple of priests, and a pair of Flemish artillery engineers. An unspecified number of the artisans and professionals invested in the company were confident enough of its outcome to bring their wives (although, following customary practice, these Spanish women probably remained with the merchants at the last Caribbean port before Yucatan was reached).

We also know the age and birthplace of more than twelve hundred conquistadors who participated in the original invasions of Panama, Mexico, Peru, and Colombia. The makeup of each expedition was similar, with an average of 30 percent from the southern Spanish kingdom of Andalusia, 19 percent from neighboring Extremadura, 24 percent from the core kingdoms of Old and New Castile, and the remainder from other regions of the Iberian peninsula. Other Europeans were rare, restricted to the odd Portuguese, Genoese, Flemish, or Greek man. In age, the conquerors ranged from teenagers to the occasional sixty-year-old; the average age of the men who went to both Peru and Colombia was twenty-seven, with the vast majority in their twenties or early thirties.

In terms of education, again the range was broad, from men who were completely illiterate and uneducated to the occasional man of considerable learning. Despite the impression given by conquistador chronicles, the fully literate were in the minority in conquest companies—although the paucity of farmers among conquistadors meant that literacy rates were slightly higher than back in Spain. Eyewitness narratives such as those by Bernal Díaz and Cortés on Mexico, and Francisco de Jérez on Peru, are classics partly because they are rare. Most conquistadors wrote or dictated "merit" reports in a formulaic style. Despite the common misconception that literacy gave Spaniards an advantage over Native Americans, members of conquistador companies could probably read and write no better than the most literate Native American societies, such as the Maya.

Nor was the correlation between social status and literacy among conquistadors as close as might be expected; the colonial chronicler Juan Rodríguez Freyle, a Bogotá native, claimed that some city council members of the New Granada settlements used branding irons to sign documents. Among the ten leaders of the famous 1532–34 invasion of Peru, including the four Pizarro brothers, four were literate, three were semiliterate (they could sign their names), and three were illiterate (including Francisco Pizarro).

Being a conquistador was not necessarily good for one´s mental health. From some perspectives, in view of the terrible risks and usually disappointing rewards, it seems a crazy vocation to choose in the first place. The sufferings, stress, and horrors of the campaigns literally drove some participants mad. Lope de Aguirre, during the expedition he led down the Amazon in 1569, slaughtered most of his companions in fits of paranoia and ended up proclaiming himself pope and emperor. Columbus and Cortés, neither of whom exhibited convincing evidence of religious feeling at the start of their careers, except at the level of rhetoric, both "got God" as a result of their hardships and embitterment: Columbus had a series of disturbing visions, in which he claimed to converse with God and experience quasi-messianic ecstasies; Cortés imagined himself as a new apostle, restoring the purity of the primitive church in a sort of relaunch of Christianity in America. The affectation, at least, of religious transports could impress some natives. Cabeza de Vaca, shipwrecked on the coast of Texas in 1528 and enslaved by locals, achieved a reputation as a holy man and—by his own account—a healer blessed with miraculous powers. Hundreds of native devotees thronged behind him when he eventually made his way overland back to New Spain after eight years of wandering.

Expanding the category

Spanish men were not the only people who fought with invading companies. The category of conquistador has traditionally been restricted to its most obvious members: those described earlier. But to fully understand Spanish conquests in the Americas, we must expand the category to include anyone who fought alongside Spanish men, to some extent or another accepting and perpetuating conquistador culture, its ethos, and its goals. This meant participating in military campaigns, pursuing the violent subjugation of native communities and the acquisition of precious metals, all with a view to settling permanently in conquered lands, forging Christian provinces of the Spanish Empire, and petitioning to be granted official rewards and privileges by the Crown in return for services rendered in the conquest. Defined thus, the conquistador category included three additional groups, discussed here in order of numerical importance: *conquistadoras*, or Spanish women conquerors (very few); black conquistadors (a significant number); and native conquistadors (very many, greatly outnumbering Spanish and black conquistadors).

Of the thousand or so Spaniards who entered Mexico in the few years following the 1519 Cortés landing, nineteen were women whose participation in the invasion justifies calling them conquistadoras. There is evidence that at least five of them actually fought. A trio of conquistadoras in South America achieved some lasting notoriety. Inés Suárez voyaged to Venezuela and Peru in search of her husband, and when she discovered he had died she joined Pedro de Valdivía's conquest company in Chile; there she became the captain's lover, fought the Araucanians, helped defend Santiago in 1541, and was awarded an encomienda in 1545. She is still remembered in Chile today. In the 1550s, doña Isabel de Guevara accompanied her husband on a campaign to conquer and settle on the Rio de la Plata, on the Mendoza expedition. She later petitioned the Crown, detailing her sacrifices and requesting an encomienda (as any conquistador would do). Finally, in her memoir of her years disguised as a man in Spanish Peru, Catalina de Erauso tells of her many battles fought against native warriors in what is today Chile and Bolivia.

The details of these examples show how they are exceptions that prove the rule: they are relatively late, none in the first wave of invasions; they took place outside the core areas of conquest and settlement; and the women in question all behaved like men, conforming to the model of the conquistador male. The rule was that conquistadors were not just men but gendered as exceptionally male, exemplars of a sixteenth-century stereotype that expected men to be bold and brash, capable of violence and cruelty in the pursuit of conquests of all kinds. Inés Suárez's most famous act was the beheading of seven native lords being held as hostages during the siege of Santiago. This was classic conquistador procedure, but it was told and retold as a courageous (and necessarily brutal) seizing of the moment when the men hesitated. The city of Santiago was named thus because the saint himself (St. James) allegedly descended on his white horse to save the day; in later accounts, Suárez rides out on a white horse, à la Santiago, to spur on the Spaniards.

Similarly, doña Isabel de Guevara wrote to Princess doña Juana, regent in Spain at the time, that as the La Plata company collapsed, the women had to act both as women and men. They carried sick men on their shoulders "with as much tenderness as if they were our own sons," but also "encouraged them with manly words." In doing so, the women were transformed into über-conquistadors:

> The men became so weak that all the tasks fell on the poor women, washing the clothes as well as nursing the men, preparing for them the little food that there was, keeping them clean, standing guard,

patrolling the fires, loading the crossbows when the Indians came sometimes to do battle, even firing the cannon, shouting the alarm through the camp, acting as sergeants and putting the soldiers in order, because at that time, as we women can make do with little nourishment, we had not fallen into such weakness as the men.

To pass as a conquistador, Catalina de Erauso had to act out the conquistador stereotype to a degree that parodied it; the conquistador par excellence. Trouble finds Erauso wherever she goes (or he goes, as Erauso is always in drag); games of cards and casual conversations regularly turn into duels and street fights, and as the body count mounts, Erauso's signature phrase "and down he went" becomes a black comic cue for the reader to chuckle. Although it is not always clear if other women have seen through Erauso's disguise, her encounters with them—playful, noncommittal, vaguely contemptuous—tend to confirm her identity as a manly conquistador. Finally, in Erauso's memoir indigenous warriors are seldom given individual identities; like the unfortunate defenders of homelands in the accounts of Cortés, Díaz, Alvarado, and Las Casas, natives are massacred with a brutal, dismissive bravado:

> Meanwhile, the Indians returned to the village more than ten thousand strong. We fell at them again with such spirit, and butchered so many of them, that blood ran like a river across the plaza, and we chased them to the Dorado River, and beyond, slaughtering all the way.

These few conquistadoras whose lives we can reconstruct in some detail do not represent a large number of other women still lost to history; conquistadoras were always relatively rare.

By contrast, the handful of black conquistadors whose biographies have been reconstructed do represent a large body of African men whose roles tended to be dismissed by Spaniards and ignored by historians. The stories of men such as Juan Valiente, Juan Garrido, and Sebastián Toral, who fought in Spanish conquest campaigns and became black conqueror-settlers, are only now being told. From the very onset, as early as the 1490s, Spaniards brought with them African slaves and servants. Their numbers increased from less than a dozen in each conquest company to many hundreds per expedition after 1521. Although black conquistadors tended to be ignored in Spanish histories of the conquests, they were not only ubiquitous but much valued as fierce fighters.

One of the black conquistadors who fought against the Aztecs and survived the destruction of their empire was Juan Garrido. Born in Africa, Garrido lived as a young slave in Portugal, before being sold to a Spaniard and acquiring his freedom fighting in the conquests of Puerto Rico, Cuba, and other islands. He fought in the Spanish-Aztec war as a free servant or auxiliary, participating in Spanish expeditions to other parts of Mexico (including Baja California) in the 1520s and 1530s. As a reward for his service, he was granted a house-plot in the new Mexico City, where he raised a family, working at times as a guard and town crier, both common occupations for black conquerors-turned-settlers. In his probanza to the king, Garrido claimed to have been the first person to plant wheat in Mexico.

Another African-born conquistador was Sebastián Toral. He had entered Yucatan as a young teenage slave owned by one of the Spanish conquistadors on the failed campaign into Yucatan of the early 1530s; he returned in 1540, possibly already free, along with the Spaniards who came to try and subdue the Maya of the peninsula for the third time. Once a colony was founded in the early 1540s, Toral worked as a guard, lived among Yucatan's new settlers as a Christian Spanish-speaker, and started a family. When a law was passed that required all those of African descent in the Spanish colonies to pay tribute, Toral wrote in protest to the king. Receiving no reply, he sailed to Spain. There he secured an order of exemption, sailing to Mexico, where he was granted a local permit to bear arms. He probably died back in Yucatan in the 1580s.

Garrido and Toral make good examples of black conquistadors for several reasons. First, as legendary war correspondent Martha Gellhorn famously observed, "war happens to people, one by one." We cannot understand the conquistador experience without identifying individuals and something of how they personally navigated their way through the conquest wars. This is as true of black as of Spanish conquistadors, and Garrido and Toral are among the few whose lives can be partially reconstructed. Second, they behaved as conquistadors—fighting Aztecs and Maya, settling in the new colonial cities, petitioning the king for recognition. Third, they remained "black," in terms of their occupations and subordinate status within the new colonies, a notch above the native peoples they had helped to conquer but never equal to the Spaniards to whom they had once been enslaved. Yet Garrido and Toral make for poor examples by virtue of their survival. Most black conquistadors did not live long enough to enjoy freedom, family, and the immortality of a place in the written record.

Last but by no means least, the title of conquistador was appropriated soon after the first wave of the conquest by Maya, Zapotec, and other indigenous elites who had allied with Spanish invaders and won certain privileges in the new colonial system. Their role was crucial, as without the many thousands of indigenous soldiers who fought as *indios amigos*, the Spanish conquistadors would not have lived to found colonies in the Americas. Native conquistadors can be viewed in two categories: those who allied with the invaders within their own lands, in order to retain some degree of local autonomy and power; and those who traveled distances to fight other native groups and settle among them.

One of the most vivid examples of the first category—especially in terms of the appropriation of the "conquistador" title—comes from Yucatan. The Pech, the royal dynasty that ruled the northwest corner of the peninsula, decided, in the face of the third Spanish invasion, to adopt an appeasement strategy. They agreed to let

Spaniards and their Nahua allies settle the Pech town of Tihó, which in 1542 was consequently "founded" as the new city of Mérida. Pech lords were baptized—taking the names of their Spanish sponsors to create hybrid monikers such as "don Francisco de Montejo Pech"—and confirmed as noblemen and rulers of the surrounding towns. They participated in campaigns against Maya in other regions of the peninsula, identifying themselves in writing as conquistadors. Nakuk Pech and Macan Pech, for example, both styled themselves in Maya-language accounts of the conquest wars as *yax hidalgos concixtador en*, combining Maya words with Spanish terms for "nobleman" and "conqueror" to mean "I, the first of the noble conquistadors."

One of the best examples of native conquistadors in the second category—those who conquered and settled abroad—are the Nahuas, or Nahuatl-speaking natives of central Mexico. Tlaxcala was (and still is) an important Nahua town, whose inhabitants—the Tlaxcalans—became famous for having resisted first Aztec and then Spanish domination. They then made an alliance with the Spanish invaders in order to help destroy the Aztec Empire, going on—ironically—to become core members of Spanish-Nahua campaigns to reconquer and extend the old empire in its new guise (see fig. 7).

The Spanish-Tlaxcala alliance took the form of a marital alliance between the Alvarado family and the royal dynasty of Xicotencatl; Pedro de Alvarado married the Tlaxcalan princess doña Luisa Xicotencatl, with whom he had two children, and Jorge de Alvarado married her sister, doña Lucía. The Alvarados took their Tlaxcalan wives, and thousands of Tlaxcalan warriors and their retinues, on their campaigns into Guatemala. Bernal Díaz remarked that "Jorge de Alvarado brought on the road with him over two hundred Indians from Tlaxcala, and [others] from Cholula, Mexicans, and from Guacachula [Quauhquechollan], and from other provinces, and they helped him in the war." The Nahua warriors also came from Xochimilco, Texcoco, and other towns in

7. Tlaxcalan conquistadors. This scene from the pictorial conquest account called the *Lienzo de Tlaxcala* depicts Tlaxcalan warriors fighting in the 1522 campaign into Michoacán in western Mexico. The expedition's leader, Nuño de Guzmán, is shown along with one other Spaniard and a Spanish mastiff, outnumbered by four Tlaxcalans in full battle plumage wielding obsidian-tipped war clubs. The charge is led not by Guzmán but the Tlaxcalan captain. The Purépecha enemy are shown resisting the invasion, but their war regalia is less impressive than that of the Tlaxcalans, and the three warriors in the frame are offset by images of fellow Purépecha being hanged and dismembered.

Central Mexico, and other ethnic groups were represented as well, such as the Mixtecs and Zapotecs of Oaxaca.

Why did Nahuas and other Mesoamericans ally with the Spaniards in such campaigns? First, Mesoamerican identity was highly localized or micropatriotic. Although Aztecs, Tlaxcalans, Quauhquechollans, the K'iche', Kaqchikel, and Pipil did indeed have much in common, such common characteristics and shared historical experiences were not enough to create a common sense of identity. Indigenous alliances across language barriers tended not to happen. Spanish leaders learned this in the 1520s, discovering that Nahua allies made conquests possible—from the fall of the Aztec Empire to the invasions of Oaxaca, Yucatan, and Guatemala.

Second, Mesoamerican city-states had learned under the Aztec Empire and during the Spanish-Aztec war that joining the imperial aggressor in an alliance preserved status, despite the loss of some autonomy as a junior partner; it also brought the protection of the expanding power, and the opportunity for advancement by joining new imperial expeditions. As one Spanish veteran conquistador put it, "some Indians from Mexico and from the province of Tlaxcala and its districts had come of their own free will to help and discover and settle the province of Guatemala, and there they stayed."

The Nahua rulers of Xochimilco, in the Valley of Mexico, insisted in a letter to the king in 1563 that they "did not make war against nor resist the Marqués del Valle [Cortés] and the Christian army." They were willing allies of Spain in the wars both against the Aztec Empire and the Guatemalan Maya:

> In addition to [fighting the Aztecs], we served Your Majesty in the conquest of Honduras and Guatemala with adelantado Alvarado, our encomendero. We gave him 2,500 warriors for the journey and all the provisions and other things necessary. As a result, those territories were won and put under the royal crown, because the Spaniards were few and poorly supplied and were going through lands where they would not have known the way if we had not shown them; a thousand times we saved them from death.

Conquistadors sought encomiendas in order to settle down and profit from native tribute and labor after the war; but they also exploited encomienda privileges in order to take conquest war elsewhere. Thus the Nahua town of Quauhquechollan was part of the encomienda held by Jorge de Alvarado. Its lords were obliged to send warriors with Jorge, but they also negotiated an agreement that granted them various privileges, protections, and exemptions, in return for a major investment of personnel in the 1527 expedition. The town's lords wrote to the Spanish viceroy in Mexico City in 1535 that they were:

> *caciques* [native rulers], lords, and principal men of the town
> of Guacachula [Quauhquechollan], descendants of the princes
> and lords of this land, and in the company of other caciques they
> helped the Spaniards to conquer and pacify much of this land with
> bows and arrows, enduring terrible wars among the barbarians
> and infidels, suffering enormous travails, placing their lives at risk
> and in danger.

Their role in the wars made Tlaxcalans and other Nahuas into conquistadors, and the privileges that they claimed reflected their expectations that they would settle as such. Yet in new Spanish-Nahua colonies in the Mexican north, in Yucatan, and in Guatemala, privileges such as exemption from paying tribute or performing manual labor were later taken away. Within a generation of the invasion the Spaniards conveniently forgot how invaluable their Nahua allies had been and began to see them as just one more "Indian" group; they lost their status as fellow invaders and colonists, reverting to being mere native subjects of the new empire.

This betrayal resulted in profound disillusionment within Nahua colonies, expressed dramatically in hundreds of petitions sent to the viceroy and the king in the late sixteenth century. In one such letter, written in 1547 in Guatemala, Tlaxcalan and Aztec veterans complained of:

> much and excessive labors, with hunger and thirst and pestilence
> and very bad treatments by our Spanish captains and their

henchmen, who forced and subjected us to violence by hanging and killing many of our people. And [although] we came with them already in peace, and to serve and help them, they made us give them slaves of war and peace, which were more than four hundred and then some more of which we have no memory, and we paid hens, corn, chili, salt, and sandals. And instead of treating us like sons and leaving us free, they made us their slaves and tributaries.

These Nahuas claimed that they were promised "allotments of Indians"—that is, their own Maya tributaries—in return for their services, but instead they themselves were divided up and allotted to Spaniards "like slaves." In other words, they expected to be treated like Spaniards, like conquistadors and encomenderos, but were instead treated like the conquered Maya—in other words, like Indians. As a bitter epitaph to the uncertain life of the native conquistador, the Tlaxcalan petitioner wrote: "And after the land was settled, we rested a little bit from the wrongdoings and mistreatments, no longer in our freedom since they brought us as servants and slaves."

Chapter 4
By a miracle of God

The conquest baffled the conquistadors.

Spaniards in sixteenth-century America puzzled over how they came to be in control of so many people over so vast an area. "When in ancient or modern times have such huge enterprises of so few succeeded against so many?" asked Francisco de Jérez, the conquistador of Peru who was the first to publish an account of the Spanish invasion of the Inca Empire. His question was partly boastful rhetoric, partly an expression of befuddled amazement. It was a genuinely surprising outcome, for Spain is, in strictly geographical terms, a poor and marginal part of Europe—and at the time Europe was, by global standards, the home continent of a backward and relatively unproductive civilization.

The most spectacular conquests were the most surprising. The states we call the Aztec and Inca empires were the fastest growing in the world in the early years of the sixteenth century. No empire of the time (with the possible exception of China) could match the Aztecs and Inca for environmental diversity or density of population. Yet Spain appeared to swallow them up. Cortés seemed perfectly justified in asserting that "Spaniards dare face the greatest peril, consider fighting their glory, and have the habit of winning." The rapidity of the process seems even more remarkable alongside the only precedent: the conquest of the few,

Stone-Age inhabitants of the Canary Islands, Spain's first overseas colony. The Canary Islanders gradually succumbed to invaders over a period of nearly a century, culminating in the subjugation of the last independent island, La Palma, in 1496. Even at that slow pace, the conquest of the islands, according to the chronicler of its closing stages, strained Spain's resources. Yet on the far side of the Atlantic, at a greater distance, facing greater numbers of foes, in more adverse circumstances, Spanish conquerors achieved startling results with astonishing speed.

Later empires, of course, achieved even more spectacular successes than Spain's in the New World. The British and French empires of the nineteenth century were bigger and more widespread. But they were the result of technological advances unavailable to conquistadors in the Americas. Rifled guns, steel cannon, steam transport, longitude-finding devices, telegraphy, quinine pills, and tropical-weight clothing: all were developments of the late eighteenth and early nineteenth centuries, when the Spanish empire was near or beyond its peak. Spain's great world empire of land and sea was strictly unparalleled as well as unprecedented. The other European empires of the time were seaborne, seaboard affairs, while those of the great Asian imperialists—the Ottomans, the Mughals in India, the Safavids in Persia, the Ming and Qing in China, the Russians in Siberia, the Uzbeks in central Asia, and the Thai in the southeast—were land-based empires with little or no seaward dimension. The Spaniards' empire covered both kinds of environment: traversing broad oceans, administering vast terrains.

The problem of Spain's ascent is broader than just one hemisphere. Spain was also remarkably successful in war in Europe, Africa, and Asia in the same period, conquering Granada, southern Navarre, Portugal, Melilla, Tangier, and much of Italy and the Philippines in the hundred years from 1480, while establishing naval ascendancy in the Atlantic and Pacific and most of the Mediterranean. Not until the 1630s did Spain's almost uniform record of victory by land and sea begin to slip into reverse. Internal peace and an ethos of service that bound the aristocracy to the Crown—while dissension rent most other Western European kingdoms—help to account for the long-sustained achievement. But the reasons for Spanish preponderance in the Old World are largely different from those for Spanish expansion in the New, where small bands of independent conquistador companies extended the frontiers with little or no help from the professional armies and navies that Spain deployed to such impressive effect in Europe.

Furthermore, that "New World" really was new to European experience. Spaniards who operated in the Americas faced repellent or intractable environments of mountains higher, forests denser, deserts broader, rains heavier, and diseases more deadly than any they knew. Hundreds of thousands of people they considered fearsome savages populated and defended these hostile lands. In many areas they horrified the newcomers with what seemed to the Spaniards to be cannibalism and human sacrifice. The conquerors were thousands of miles from home, and typically operated without hope of help from their fellow countrymen; indeed, because the conquests were private enterprises, the conquerors were often in competition and sometimes in conflict with each other.

So how could they succeed, against all these odds? How did Spaniards themselves explain their success?

Interior strength

In sixteenth-century New Spain and Peru, colonists who looked back on the conquests of the Aztec and Inca empires explained them, broadly speaking, in two ways. Some writers of surviving accounts—especially priests—saw Spanish triumph as providentially ordained to procure the conversion of the native peoples and perhaps to prepare for the end of the world. Gaspar de Marquina, writing from Cajamarca in 1533 of the capture of Atahualpa, explained that "we took this lord by a miracle of God, because our forces wouldn't be enough to take him nor to do what we did, but God gave us the victory miraculously over him and his forces." The difficulties of the conquests and their dazzling rewards made them explicable in divine terms, as a kind of miracle, signified by miraculous attendants: battlefield-apparitions of the Virgin Mary and Santiago (St. James), Spain's patron saint. The conquest was providential; God had ordained it, using Spaniards as his agents to bring the true faith and the benefits of civilization to the pagan barbarians of the New World. As a result, in Spanish eyes there was something miraculous about military triumphs over great empires such as those of the Aztecs and Inca.

Alongside this providential explanation, which assigned the greater role to God and the humbler role to the conquistadors themselves—*non nobis, Domine, sed nomini tuo sit Gloria* (Not to us, Lord, . . . but to your name be glory given)—was another, which, though contradictory, could be espoused by some of the same people. This further explanation ascribed the conquest to some supposed form of Spanish superiority, usually superior prowess or morale. Bernardo de Vargas Machuca, in his lengthy 1599 treatise on how conquistadors should fight, called the alleged phenomenon of superior morale "interior strength." Pizarro won Peru owing "to the persistence of interior strength." If Cortés "had possessed only exterior strength, lacking interior strength, he would have ended up losing the empire, so great and so rich, that he won by strength of spirit." As for Jiménez de Quesada:

> What was it that placed such a distinguished and wealthy kingdom in his hands? Interior fortitude, for although with exterior strength he broke through so much forest undergrowth and suffered innumerable labors, at the end, force of spirit fed this strength in such a manner that he never lost heart amid such adversities and deaths of many of his soldiers from hunger.

This was, clearly, a self-interested theory of explanation. Conquistadors—like all seekers of preferment under the Spanish monarchy in the early modern period—had to petition the Crown for pay and privileges, specifying their services (as we saw earlier). Many surviving conquistador narratives of the conquest consisted or originated in documents of this kind, which of course exaggerated the petitioners' achievements. A case in point is the memorandum Hernán Sánchez de Badajoz drew up, relating the part he played at the siege of Cuzco, during the conquest of the Inca, in 1536. By his own account, he captured a tower single-handedly by breaking down the gate, killing all the defenders at ground level, shimmying up a rope under a hail of rocks, and killing the defenders on the ramparts. This simply defied credibility. But the distortions of memory, allied with the agendas of the narrators, made such claims commonplace in the literature; they were central to the culture of the genre. Even if we allow that the conquistadors were men of exceptional daring and strength (a big "if"), their endowment of valor can hardly have made up for the disparities in numbers they faced or the toll of the hardships they endured.

The idea that the Spaniards enjoyed superior morale is more attractive. An image early colonial writers invented to support it— that of native peoples cowed by their own doom-fraught oracles, abandoning resistance under the influence of omens of their undoing, or in the conviction that their enemies were gods—has helped to convince subsequent generations that the Aztecs, and perhaps other Native Americans too, were victims of their own corroded morale. Even the great present-day historian of the early modern Atlantic world, J. H. Elliott, in his youth asserted that Spanish conquests were made possible by military superiority and "the greater self-confidence of the civilization that produced the conquistadors."

The supposed basis for the assumption is mythical. It is simply nonsensical that the Aztecs or Inca could have mistaken the Spaniards for divine beings. There is no evidence for such a view traceable to native sources. Other cases of the occurrence of myths of returning gods or "gods from the sea" or of the advent of beings "from beyond the horizon" occur among coastal and island peoples, not inland, highland imperialists, though the latter did tend, in Mesoamerica, to honor heroes and visiting dignitaries with divine forms of address. The behavior of native hosts toward the Spaniards was always—within native traditions—commensurate and appropriate for human guests.

Likewise, the omens that supposedly preceded the fall of the Aztecs' city of Tenochtitlán are a pure deception. All the alleged omens were drawn, sometimes with slight modifications, from three works with no indigenous pedigree: Plutarch's *Lives*, Lucan's *Pharsalia*, and the *History of the Jews* by Josephus. These texts were all part of the classical curriculum, taught in early colonial Mexico in the Franciscan College of Santa Cruz de Tlatelolco, where the story of the omens first appeared in the 1540s. All tell of the fates of Rome and Jerusalem. For the young scions of Nahua nobility educated in the college, Tenochtitlán was their Rome and their Jerusalem. Naturally they lamented its fall with images drawn from the literature they studied. Their teachers treated these reconstructions of the past as if they were genuine memories.

Furthermore, there is no evidence that the Aztecs were particularly prone to subversion by superstition. Every fifty-two years they rekindled the sacred fire that nourished the cosmos and without which the world would supposedly end. But in every society, such rites outlive the beliefs they embody. Aztec success in dealing with the natural world—in agriculture, in building, in organizing for war—suggests rationally informed competence, not magically inhibited minds. In any case, the fire-kindling ceremony had last been completed in 1507, only a decade before the conquistadors arrived. So if the natives were disposed to believe in the imminent end of the world, they would have to acknowledge that it was still many years off.

On the other hand, evidence of shaky Spanish morale abounds. Fear comes through the dry-mouthed accounts of witnesses of human sacrifices. The same emotion probably prompted the massacres and terror-tactics to which the Spaniards resorted spasmodically. When the conquistador Bernal Díaz penned the most famous description of Tenochtitlán, likening it to an enchanted castle in a popular romance of chivalry, the kind of enchantment he had in mind was diabolic sorcery, and the castle he invoked was a horrendous, grim, gaunt, dark, and terrible place. There is no reason to think the natives were more afraid of the Spaniards than the Spaniards were of the natives. The tenacity of native resistance is a strong indicator of robust morale. Though most literature on the subject represents the conquests of Mexico and Peru as quick and easy, the reverse is true. Tenochtitlán resisted ferociously, even when the fight seemed hopeless by any normal calculations. The Inca, when their heartlands fell, continued resistance in the mountain valleys, where they maintained an independent kingdom until 1572.

Yet historians have tended to take the Spanish-generated stories of their superiority at face value and even to add to them. Most of the historical literature represents the Spaniards as advantaged not only in morale and prowess, but also in technology, political sophistication, and metabolic resistance.

Take technology first. As detailed in the previous chapter, Spaniards had "guns and steel," but it is doubtful whether these really conferred an advantage. Guns are good only as long as powder and shot can be replaced. Even crossbows need supplies of bolts. Heavy armor is an encumbrance in rarefied atmospheres and hot climates—indeed, the Spaniards rapidly discarded steel cuirasses and heavy leather jerkins for the quilted cotton armor of the Aztecs and other Mesoamericans. Images of conquistadors in full armor were mostly created after the events, reflecting the battle dress of later generations of European soldiers (see figs. 2–8).

Horses, Spain's other supposed secret weapon, extinct in the Americas for ten thousand years before Spaniards reintroduced them, were much loved by Spaniards as a status symbol, and they seem to have captured native imaginations. But they were of little use in mountainous terrain and street fighting of the kind decisive in most of Mesomerica and the Andes. Pedro de Alvarado's complaints that in Guatemala at times "the horses were not able to keep up the lead owing to the roughness of the road" and "the horsemen could not fight on account of the many marshes and thick forests" were common refrains. In the earlier campaigns, horseshoes became a rare and valued commodity, as without them horses went from being a help to a hindrance; Alvarado wrote in 1524 from Guatemala that horseshoes "are now worth among us 190 pesos a dozen and so we are trading them and paying for them in gold." Horses could be used to devastating effect on open plains, and Spanish accounts of conquest battles are full of descriptions of efforts to lure enemy warriors onto an open field—and of the slaughter that ensued if they were successful. But such moments serve to illustrate the limitation of horses in general. Furthermore, native warriors soon learned to avoid open battles, to hamstring horses or pull them down by their tails, and to dig hidden pits of sharpened stakes to impale horses and their riders. Natives also learned to ride horses themselves readily enough.

The really significant technology at the Spaniards' disposal was nautical. Their ships got them to the New World in the first place—an achievement no indigenous seafarers could match in the opposite direction. And they were able to extemporize suitable craft for river and lake warfare. But this advantage, though critical in some places, such as central Mexico where assailants had to approach the Aztec stronghold of Tenochtitlán across a lake, was obviously of limited application.

Belief that Spaniards were more adept politically than the natives is unlikely to infest an impartial mind. On the contrary, Spanish success occurred in spite of conquistadors' political ineptitude. Neither Cortés in Mexico nor Pizarro and his brothers in Peru ever understood the political institutions of their enemies. Cortés thought he was dealing with a centralized monarchy, which he could control by capturing and manipulating the Aztec emperor—standard practice in the Caribbean since the 1490s, in the Canaries before that, and in the Iberian peninsula before that. The results were disillusioning. The Aztecs simply ceased to take notice of their ruler once he was in Spanish hands. Pizarro, failing to grasp the realities of the Conquest of Mexico, tried the same strategy—partially because it was Spanish convention, and partially in imitation of Cortés. It worked rather better in Peru, but by accident. In both areas, the Spaniards were successful in recruiting native communities to their side, but not as a result of any skill of their own. Native intermediaries negotiated the alliances—necessarily so, since only they spoke the relevant languages. For most of their dealings, outside the Maya linguistic area, where there were Spaniards who spoke some of the languages, invaders were compelled in the early stages of the conquests to rely on linguistically proficient interpreters—usually captives—who learned Spanish quickly.

It is true, finally, that people from the Old World brought unfamiliar diseases to the New and that unimmunized natives died in the hundreds of thousands, perhaps millions, from the effects, especially of smallpox, in the early colonial period. The only way to become immune was to catch and then survive the disease—which most indigenous sufferers did not. As the frontier of European penetration advanced, throughout the colonial centuries, the pattern was repeated. In this respect, Europeans did enjoy an advantage that might be termed a type of superiority: they were naturally immune to the diseases they introduced. However, disease cannot itself explain the outcome of the invasions, and it is important to emphasize that the havoc plague wrought did not necessarily undermine native resistance. Four considerations make caution advisable in reckoning the impact of disease on the conquest.

First, the chronology of the outbreaks of disease did not always match the pace of conquest. In Peru, certainly, smallpox preceded the Spaniards and therefore may have helped them. In Mexico, however, though afflictions usual in the circumstances assailed Tenochtitlán under siege—including typhus, probably, and perhaps starvation—the evidence of when smallpox first struck is equivocal. In some places, demographic disaster did not set in until after the conquistadors had moved on, unwittingly spreading disease through the indigenous world. Second, despite the deadly sweep of disease, the defenders of Mexico and Peru were able to field armies scores of thousands strong. Disease does not necessarily enfeeble resistance; sometimes, the more deadly the threat, the tougher the defenders' resolve. This was apparently the case in Tenochtitlán in 1520–21, as it was in the seventeenth century when the Iroquois of the Great Lakes region of North America faced French invaders whom they correctly associated with the spread of smallpox. Third, and decisively, conquest almost always relied more on huge indigenous armies, mobilized in support of the conquistadors, than on Spanish manpower. The native allies were at least as vulnerable to Spanish-borne disease as the resisters, who, of course, were remoter from the source of infection. Disease, as far as it was effective at all, worked against conquest as much as in its favor. Finally, though Spaniards were immunized against European diseases, they found American environments extremely hostile. They were not acclimatized, for instance, to the altitudes of the Aztec and Inca heartlands and were vulnerable to the malaria common in the lowlands they had to traverse.

If neither the conquistadors themselves nor the historians who followed them had convincing explanations of what happened in the conquest, what about the natives themselves?

By force of arms

In early colonial records authentic indigenous voices are hard to distinguish from those of the Spanish priests and officials who recorded them and influenced them. Most native elites became collaborators in the colonial regime and accepted or even crafted its myths. Mid to late sixteenth-century laments, for instance, over the fall of the Mexican city of Tenochtitlán-Tlatelolco have often been taken for genuine Aztec threnodies, but they seem suspiciously like poems in European and Islamic traditions that would have been familiar to Spaniards of the time. Historians who took at face value the stories about the supposed portents that predisposed the Aztecs to failure, or about the natives' supposed identification of Spaniards as divine, were evidently victims of their own credulity and of the tendency of early colonial-period natives to reflect the culture, traditions, and beliefs of the conquerors. Reminiscences of these kinds, filtered through the values of classical humanism and recasting the preconquest states as similar to those of ancient Greeks and Romans, multiplied in the late sixteenth and seventeenth centuries.

Some Maya noblemen in colonial Yucatan, recalling the era of the conquest, identified so completely with the Spaniards as to call themselves "noble conquistadors." Rather than lament the invasion, they evinced pride in the role they claimed in the introduction of Christianity to their benighted brethren. In Peru, an Inca leader, who ruled the independent native state in the forests of Vilcabamba, subscribed to the providential view of the conquest, writing about it as if it were an act of divine chastisement of his predecessors. Meanwhile, in Spain, an Inca prince who became a respected man of letters, praised Inca imperialism as equivalent to Rome's. In the 1560s and 1570s, the viceroy of Peru made leaders of indigenous communities listen and assent to long historical lectures presenting a Spanish account of the conquest as a liberation from Inca tyranny. As various as these versions of the past were, they all derived as much from Spanish as from native traditions.

Nevertheless, a few sources can be said to embody native views, uncorrupted (though never entirely uninfluenced) by Spanish agendas. In the aftermath of the conquest, indigenous leaders and communities had to petition the Crown for rewards and privileges just as Spaniards did. Their petitions sometimes convey priorities very different from those of the Spanish conquistadors. At times, they lay claim to a version of the conquest that is patently untrue, yet which nonetheless reveals something of indigenous perspectives. For example, a half-century after the Spanish invasion of Guatemala, the Tz'utijil Maya rulers of Atitlán wrote to King Philip II that:

> When don Pedro de Alvarado and the other Spanish conquistadors came to these parts, when they invaded all these lands, no town surrendered in peace but only by force of arms; and having arrived at our town of Santiago de Atitlán, they received don Pedro and the others in the spirit of good friendship and certainly without any of them taking up arms.

A dozen Spanish sources undermine in detail the Tz'utijil claim to have welcomed Alvarado with open arms. The evidence is strong that, to the contrary, the Tz'utijils put up brief but brave resistance to a massive invasion force of Spaniards, Nahuas, and Kaqchikel; as their one-time enemies and neighbors, the Kaqchikel, commented, "the Tz'utijils then died because of the Castilians." So why deny that noble fact? The answer lies in the nature of the 1571 Tz'utijil letter to the king; the document is a petition requesting a reduction in tribute to local Spanish officials, and the claim to an original, unblemished loyalty is clearly designed to serve that purpose. Yet we cannot assume that Tz'utijil rulers deliberately lied; it is possible that local tradition had erased the memory of that initial resistance to the invaders. In other words, one indigenous explanation for the conquest was that it never happened: the Spaniards arrived, they were welcomed, Christianity was adopted, life went on.

At the same time, the Tz'utijil summary of the brutal invasion wars of the 1520s is revealing in another way. For all accounts of the Guatemalan story—be they Nahua, Maya, or Spanish—support the notion that nobody surrendered except "by force of arms" (as the Tz'utijils assert was the case everywhere else in the region). Therein lies another indigenous explanation: invaders came; we fought them; the wars wore us down. As the Kaqchikel account of Alvarado's invasion comments, "we began to be killed again by the Castilians; they were opposed again by the people. They waged war for a long time, and again they were absorbed by death."

Not that such laments eclipse the crucial role played by native micropatriotism (that is, the highly localized nature of indigenous identity). In the midst of the Kaqchikel description of the war against them, the Kaqchikel still boast of how they "distinguished themselves"—even more so than "the Castilians"—in the destruction of the neighboring kingdoms of the K'iche' and Tz'utijil Maya. Likewise, in Mexico, micropatriotism was paramount. The leaders of Huejotzinco and Tlaxcala disputed Aztec hegemony in central Mexico before the conquest and allied with the Spaniards during it. Sources from both towns present a coherent and not unpersuasive view of the conquest as the work of some indigenous communities fighting others. In their own eyes, the Tlaxcalans and Huejotzincans were the real conquerors of Mexico.

A set of Tlaxcalan submissions now known as the *Lienzo de Tlaxcala* are of particular interest because they chronicle the conquest in pictorial form (see fig. 7). A succession of vivid representations of battles show Tlaxcalan soldiers in the vanguard, doing all the actual fighting, while the Spaniards discreetly bring up the rear (like Gilbert and Sullivan's Duke of Plaza Toro, who "led from behind" because "he found it less exciting").

This native view is as self-interested as the conquistadors' accounts of their own heroism. But it is, perhaps, slightly more plausible. If natives did most of the fighting, it would help to explain the relatively low casualties—at least, low fatal casualties—the Spaniards tended to suffer. Likewise, it helps to account for the relatively small numbers captured for sacrifice (for in the Mesoamerican tradition of warfare, especially in central Mexico, the tally of captives was more important than the tally of casualties, and the object of battle was to feed the altars of sacrifice).

Moreover, the *Lienzo de Tlaxcala* presents a convincing account of the way the Spaniards recruited native help. In all the scenes of negotiation of alliances, the central role is played by Cortes's native interpreter, whom the Spaniards called doña Marina. She was a native speaker of Nahuatl—the lingua franca of central Mexico— whom the conquistadors had liberated from enslavement on their march to Mexico. Since, on all these occasions, she was the only person present who understood everything everybody said, she was in a uniquely privileged position, able to forge alliances for her own purposes and manipulate events to her will. Her exact provenance is unknown, but she must obviously have belonged to one of the peoples subject to the Aztec hegemony and resentful of the levels of tribute they had to pay the empire. She bore a child by Cortés nine months after the fall of Tenochtitlán and thus eventually came to be viewed derisively as his mistress. But that theme is absent from native accounts, and in the *Lienzo*, doña Marina enjoys a further role as the presiding genius of the entire conquest, directing operations in battle, while Cortés assumes an ancillary place. Other communities who allied with the Spaniards seem similarly to have treated her as the real leader or joint leader of the invaders.

From a present-day perspective, it is tempting to read the *Lienzo de Tlaxcala* and similar sources as descriptions of internecine conflict among indigenous peoples—a sort of Native American civil war. Yet participants would not have seen it that way. The very concept of a Native American was alien to indigenous peoples at the time; nor did Mesoamericans or Andeans share a common identity. Only after centuries of colonial presence and interactions with a wider world did regional ethnic identities emerge, let alone a hemispheric native identity. Before, during, and for several centuries after the time of the Spanish invasions, native identities were highly localized. No one in the Americas can have felt any sense of transcendent unity. Rival communities occupied the hemisphere and fought each other for resources. What we call the conquest was for them—at least, when it started and in many cases for generations afterwards—just another episode in their long history of mutual hostility.

In central Mexico there were two levels of division: disunity among the incumbent elites; and a detestation of the hegemonic peoples that enflamed intercommunal war. The people we call the Aztecs inhabited a precariously allied group of city-states, most of which were located on islands in or shores around Lake Texcoco, more than seven thousand feet high in the midst of the central valley. At this altitude and in this environment, it was impossible to grow cotton, which the Aztecs needed for their clothing and battle armor. Nor could the region produce the elite goods needed for the ritual life of the leaders, such as rubber for the ball game, which was an essential form of aristocratic exercise as well as a sacred cult; or cacao for their heady, theobromine-intense ritual tipple; or incense for their religious rites; or exotic feathers for their headdresses. In a lake-bound city like Tenochtitlán, they could not even grow enough food—in the form of the staple beans and maize on which everyone depended to sustain life—in the terrain available. So these cities were self-condemned to a life of predation. The elite of Tenochtitlán represented their city as an eagle's eyrie, surrounded by the blood and bones of its victims. An elaborate network of tribute crisscrossed the Aztec culture-area, culminating in Tenochtitlán and vexing most other cities. Demands for human-sacrifice victims increased the burden on tributary states. These demands were considerable. Early colonial sources claim variously that the hearts of between twenty thousand and eighty thousand living human victims were ripped out to hallow the main temple of Tenochtitlán when it was consecrated in 1487; even twenty thousand is surely an exaggeration, but the event was clearly recalled for generations as one of fearsomely bloody excess. It would be impertinent to suppose that the many communities that united to oppose the Aztecs envisaged a reward of the kind the Spaniards brought. Presumably, they wanted a redistribution of tribute in a way favorable to themselves. For them, the outcome was an instance of the law of unforeseen consequences.

In Yucatan, the predominance of elite disunity emerges strongly from the petitions and narratives, made for posterity, of the self-proclaimed native conquistadors, and from the books of mingled history and prophecy, written in the colonial era in a precolonial tradition and known as the *Books of Chilam Balam* (or *Jaguar Prophet*). Contending noble lineages—of which the most notable were the Xiu, Pech, and Cocom—had disputed hegemony in the region for centuries. The most traumatic, bloody, destructive, and vividly remembered incidents of their wars occurred before the Spaniards arrived. When they elected to support or oppose the Spaniards, they made their choices on the basis of long nourished hatreds and long remembered resentments.

The Maya of Yucatan were divided into very loosely defined kingdoms at the time of the Spanish invasion—historians have traditionally referred to them simply as independent "provinces." This made for a fluid political scene, in which Maya rulers broke alliances with each other and with the Spaniards as quickly as they made them. By the time the major fighting was over, in 1547—after two long decades—Spaniards still only controlled the peninsula's northwest. The border would move slowly east and south over the centuries, but Spain would never control the whole peninsula. Thus native disunity made the Conquest of Yucatan a protracted, bloody, and geographically incomplete affair. But it also made it possible; had the Maya dynastic elite united against the invaders, they might have been able to repel them indefinitely.

The situation among Maya to the south, in highland Guatemala, was slightly different, in ways that are illuminating. There was no single empire, whose resentful provincial leaders could be won over to the invaders' cause (as in central Mexico), or whose well-built infrastructure could be taken over by the Spaniards (as in the Andes). Nor was there a scattering of small kingdoms, more or less equal in power, forcing the Spaniards to make military forays and local alliances over and over (as in Yucatan). Instead, there were two larger kingdoms in the highlands, surrounded by smaller polities extending north into the lowlands and south to the Pacific coast. The two larger kingdoms were those of the K'iche' (Quiché) and Kaqchiquel (Cakchiquel) Maya. The K'iche' had once dominated the Kaqchiquel, but the latter had rebelled fifty years before the Spaniards arrived. Since the revolt the two had maintained a rivalry so intense that even in the face of a brutal Spanish-led assault on their homelands they failed to establish a working alliance.

One might assume that empires would fall less easily than small kingdoms, and thus the larger the polity the more trouble it gave the Spaniards. Counterintuitively, the opposite was the case. Because if the complex nature of native disunity, the large empire of the Aztecs fell after a two-year war, the dominant kingdoms of highland Guatemala came under Spanish control after five years of bloodshed, and the dozen small polities of northern Yucatan were "pacified" after twenty years of invasions. The dating of these wars—1519–21, 1524–29, and 1527–47, respectively—reveals a further dimension to the comparison. Spanish success after 1521 was based not only on the fact that the Aztec capital of Tenochtitlán had been utterly destroyed and its royal family killed or captured. It was also based on the rapid way in which Spaniards, Aztecs, and the elite of other Nahua city-states in central Mexico adapted the old empire to the new; combined Spanish-Nahua forces "reconquered" the Aztec empire as the kingdom of New Spain. The success of this technique was such that by the late 1520s, Spanish-Nahua forces had breached the old imperial boundaries of the Aztecs and invaded Maya lands. Campaigns into Guatemala and Yucatan led by the Alvarados and Montejos would surely have failed completely were it not for the thousands of Nahuas and other Mesoamerican warriors that comprised the bulk of the invasion companies.

In Peru, in an Inca world riven by internal rivalries, native sources reveal a similar accumulation of resentment on the part of subject communities. The Inca practiced what we might call ecological imperialism. In the Andean region, the precipitate landscape, which streaks between tropical forest and sea, crams a stunning diversity of environments into relatively small areas. On two sides of a mountain, or in adjacent valleys, contrasting patterns of rain and sun prevail. As one ascends the slopes, humidity, temperature and prevalent biota change within a short space. Marine and lowland products are available from relatively close at hand. Therefore, almost all large Andean states, for centuries before the Inca ascent, had exploited this diversity, combining the products of different zones to enhance the richness of life.

The Inca did nothing new in this respect—except that they did it on a vastly bigger scale than any of their predecessors. Their armies ranged over thousands of miles and some thirty degrees of latitude, adding north–south diversity to the upslope–downslope, east–west kinds of diversity familiar in earlier periods. As well as shunting produce across their empire, they shifted whole populations to labor in environments where expanded production was required. When, for instance, the Inca conquered the rival, coastal state of Chimor in the late fifteenth century, they razed the main city virtually to the ground and deported the entire population. In the years before the Spaniards arrived, the ruler Huayna Capac was said to have transferred many thousands of laborers from all over the empire to work the fields of Cochabamba, planting coca to grace or madden the rituals of the Inca élite. He supposedly impressed scores of thousands more to build his summer palace. Terror tactics were as much the purpose as ecological efficiency. Huayna Capac reputedly put twenty thousand enemy warriors to death by drowning in Lake Yahyar-Cocha when he conquered the Canari.

There were therefore constituencies ready and eager to contest Inca hegemony. But resentments of subtler kinds were also at work. For instance, one of the most revealing sources, compiled in the late sixteenth or very early seventeenth centuries, records traditions of the Checa, a people of the Huarochirí valley, which occupied a strategic position in early colonial times on the road from Lima—the capital the Spaniards built—to the former Inca stronghold of Cuzco. The boundaries of the Checas' priorities were narrowly defined. They were almost always in conflict with their neighbors, whom they feared as rivals or despised as "savages," and had attained local supremacy, thanks in part to an alliance with the Inca. Shortly before the Spaniards arrived, however, the Inca had broken the terms of the agreement by refusing to perform an annual dance at the Checas' principal shrine. Such were the forms of Andean political life, signified by rituals unintelligible to the Spaniards. In revulsion from this insult, the Checa joined the alliance that overthrew their former friends.

Subsequent extensions of the territory Spain ruled also relied on native allies. The armies the Spaniards led into Guatemala and Honduras in the 1520s were formed largely of Nahuatl-speaking warriors. The same was still true of the soldiery that conquered New Mexico for Spain in the last years of the sixteenth century. So one way of understanding what happened in what we call the conquest is to see the Spaniards as the surprise beneficiaries of unsurprising processes: renewed episodes in a familiar history, characteristic of the wars of indigenous peoples, which from time to time displaced existing supremacies and erected new hegemonies.

Whatever the merits of this picture, it raises further problems. First, why did the Spaniards—who were numerically the least potent of the allies in the overthrow of the Aztecs and Inca, and who were interlopers and outsiders throughout the lands they came to rule in the New World—benefit from the changes they witnessed, rather than any of the indigenous contenders? Why, for instance, did Tlaxcalan supremacy not succeed that of the Aztecs? Why did the Inca realm not simply break up into a number of native-led states? Why were there so few places, within the penumbra of the Aztec and Inca worlds and in much of the rest of the Americas, where Spanish rule was rejected? Moreover, this native-centric or indigenist interpretation overlooks a fact of cardinal importance: what we call the conquest is largely misnamed. In most places, there was no conquest at all.

Explaining it away

Consider this claim for a moment. Traditionally, the bloody and terrible story of the establishment of European hegemony in the Americas has dominated historians' thinking about the subject. War—as the novelist Thomas Hardy once said—makes "rattling good history, but peace is poor reading." Because so many sources take the form of warriors' claims to merit, they dwell on battles and communicate a picture of intense conflict. After the conquest, a strong lobby of critics of imperialism in Spain denounced their fellow countrymen for cruelties and barbarities, confirming the impression of horrible violence. When we think of the conquests of Mexico and Peru, for instance, images leap to mind of the massacre Cortés inflicted on at least three thousand peaceful inhabitants of the city of Cholula, or of the incident at Cajamarca, when Pizarro captured the Inca emperor by—in effect—slaughtering many of his three thousand virtually unarmed attendants in an unprovoked attack. But these were eye-catching episodes, desperate expedients by desperate men, resorting to terror in trauma-sickened isolation, to relieve their fears or *pour encourager les autres*. The conventional story of the Conquest of Mexico traces the outline of three wars: the Spaniards' trial of strength against the Tlaxcalans, prior to their alliance; the bloody struggle for Tenochtitlán; and the brutal reduction of Michoacán, north of the valley of Mexico, when the inhabitants broke with the Spaniards after an initial accommodation, and provoked merciless revenge. The remarkable feature of these conflicts, however, is generally unremarked: that there were so few of them.

The contest with the Tlaxcalans was a kind of test of the Spaniards' fitness as potential allies, not a genuinely hostile action on the natives' part. The violence in the other two episodes was real enough. But the Aztecs and the peoples of Michoacán were only two groups out of many hundreds in the region. None of the others had to be coerced into submission. Typically, they came to peaceful accommodations with the Spaniards. In some parts of what became Spain's New World empire, no passage of arms was necessary: adherence to the Spanish monarchy was negotiated by unarmed priests or ambassadors. The Spanish empire, though by no means the most brutal or ill-intentioned in human history, was a terrible affliction for most of the peoples who endured it, and its malign effects are obvious. But it must be acknowledged that in most of its territory its establishment was remarkably peaceful. At the very least, we have to find an explanation of "conquest" that takes the dearth of conquests and the plethora of relatively little-contested negotiations and accommodations into account.

One of the most conspicuous trends in the recent historical writings on empires restores long-excluded realism to our picture of how empires work. It is extremely rare for one community to subjugate another without indigenous quislings and collaborators. Before industrialization, which equipped modern states with staggeringly efficient resources of communication and armories of coercion, it was impossible to effect enduring conquests on unwilling victims. Native peoples under colonial rule rarely, if ever, forfeited all power and initiative, but went on shaping their own histories inside the frameworks of the empires to which they belonged. In modern times, the great empires erected by British, French, Dutch and to some extent German conquerors all practiced what the British called "indirect rule"—leaving or devolving power to indigenous elites. Typically, they recruited their armies and police forces from native ranks. We should not expect an early-modern empire like Spain's to be any different. Indeed, if anything, it must have been even more reliant on native intermediaries, because of the vastness of the territories that comprised it, the paucity of resources that sustained it, the shortage of Spanish manpower from which it always suffered, the "tyranny of distance," and the difficulty of communications that made control elusive.

The evidence bears out these reflections. That leaves the problem of how to fathom the motives of the peoples who confided authority to the Spaniards and in most cases continued to endure Spanish rule, paying tribute and cooperating in their own exploitation, remarkably unrestively. Cultures hospitable to the Spaniards all exhibited the stranger-effect; that is, they traditionally valued the stranger and had a predisposition to accord him honor. Some anthropologists contend that all societies at some stages of development privilege the stranger, and even that all monarchies originate in the elevation of strangers as kings. However that may be, there are plenty of societies, especially in southeast Asia and the Pacific, that have evinced this tendency in recent times, when it has been meticulously documented. Even for modern Westerners, who have no active tradition of deference to strangers, this is intelligible, because we value exotic commodities, just as other cultures value exotic individuals. The anthropologist Mary Helms has gathered innumerable instances of societies that literally hallow goods in proportion to the distance they travel, and in terms of the proximity of their supposed provenance to the divine horizon. People acquire sanctity or some lesser form of respectability in the same way. In the documented history of the West, pilgrims earned veneration and travelers returned from afar with enhanced reputations for wisdom.

The prevalence of bias toward the stranger in many Native American traditions is of a piece with these familiar instances. Conceivably, this is the key to understanding the Spaniards' claims to be mistaken for gods. They were received in many places with the kind of reverence due not to gods but to gods' gifts, invested with mystery by virtue of coming from afar. The role of missionaries in advancing the frontiers of empire becomes intelligible in this connection: it is easy to defer to a holy man whose very provenance is made sacred by its remoteness.

In any case, in some social and political contexts, the stranger is a godsend of an entirely practical sort. Unencumbered by links to any existing factions, power centers, or rival lineages, the stranger makes an ideal arbiter in every kind of dispute. The power of arbitration is a kind of judicial authority, which in most societies is a function—and often is the defining ingredient—of sovereignty. In many places in Mesoamerica and the Andes, lay Spaniards and priests found roles in settling native disputes over land, kingship, and the distribution of wealth and power. With every arbitration, Spaniards became more valuable to their host societies and more entrenched as part of, or additional to, the traditional power structures. Exoticism is, to some tastes, sexually attractive; and many societies routinely practice sexual hospitality to strangers. But practical considerations also urge the choice of stranger as marriage partner, especially for members of elites, precisely because marriage to an insider tends to compromise one's political independence, whereas the stranger confers prestige without encumbering his or her spouse with embarrassing affiliations. That is why even in Europe royal families have typically sought marriage partners from outside their realms. It is not surprising that so many indigenous dynasties in the Americas should have done the same with the Spaniards. When stranger-marriage (or some less formal kind of cohabitation) occurs, consequences follow. The stranger typically acquires authority, services, tribute, ritual deference, a place of honor and even of power in the host society. The characteristic forms of economic exploitation, by which Spaniards were maintained in the early colonial period, were of kinds acquired almost automatically by virtue of their alliances with high-status native women. Spanish imperium, though violently acquired in some places, was in others a consequence of the stranger-effect.

Does this model of empowerment by virtue of the stranger-effect help explain conquests by people beyond the Spanish frontier in

America? The most suggestive cases are almost always left out of the literature: the maroon kingdoms frequently established by runaway slaves, sometimes in communities of their own but also over indigenous peoples. The processes that elevated slaves to power over natives were also, a fortiori, capable of empowering Spaniards. English, French, Portuguese, and Dutch colonists also operated at times in places subject to the stranger-effect. Usually, invaders of those nationalities modeled their enterprises on Spanish precedents. They gained footholds by exploiting the welcome natives offered them, acquiring rights of settlement, for example, in Dutch Manhattan and English Pennsylvania by peaceful negotiation. The pilgrim settlers in Massachusetts and the ne'er-do-wells who established the first enduring English colony in Virginia would have starved to death in the early days of their efforts if the natives had not fed them. Invaders all over the Americas exploited existing rivalries and divisions among the natives to recruit collaborators and make alliances, just as the Spaniards did in the Americas. Although no other colonists were as adept as Spaniards in sexual politics, alliances with native women sometimes reinforced good, or at least exploitable, relationships.

There is an intriguing irony here—that Spaniards survived in the Americas in the short term because they were strangers, and in the long run because they were locals. The stranger-effect helps to explain why Spaniards were so often the beneficiaries of internecine indigenous wars. It accounts for the extension of Spanish power by negotiation and accommodation. It contributes to our understanding of the violent episodes of conquest by enhancing the context in which the recruitment of indigenous allies becomes intelligible. The outcome of those violent episodes, however, is too big and various a phenomenon to yield to a single, all-encompassing explanation. How, in the words of Jérez, did "such huge enterprises of so few succeed against so many"? For a complete understanding—or as close to one as we can come—we must return to basics and allow that, while none of the traditional explanations we have anatomized in the preceding pages is satisfactory on its own, many of them have a place as part of an armory of explanations, the balance of which may shift—along with the cultural context and environmental conditions—from one part of the Americas to another.

First, even allowing for the impact of disease, the conquistadors were greatly outnumbered among sedentary societies such as the Aztecs and other Nahua, the Maya, and the Andeans. This numerical imbalance was largely offset by indigenous micropatriotism. The highly localized nature of Native American identities fostered native disunity. This made possible the Spanish recruitment of large numbers of native warriors under their own leaders, the acquisition of native interpreters (of whom doña Marina is the most famous), and the collaboration of indigenous élites in conquest campaigns and colony building.

Spanish weaponry was not a decisive advantage, capable alone of explaining Spanish success. But it gave the conquistadors a fighting chance at survival. The weapon that killed more native warriors and saved invaders more often than any other was the steel sword. Of secondary importance were guns, horses, and war dogs or mastiffs; these were not available to all Spaniards and were useful only under particular circumstances, although Spaniards greatly prized horses.

Despite the benefit to Spaniards of epidemic disease, native allies, and the steel blade, there remained moments in the history of the conquest when the invaders perished anyway—and moments when they would have perished were it not for the very circumstances of the Spanish invasion. Spanish invaders risked nothing beyond their own skins. Pressing on held the promise of great wealth and social prestige; turning back assured debt, ignominy, and perhaps the retribution of a betrayed patron. Native leaders, in contrast, were defending more than their lives. At stake were the lives of their families, the future status of their descendents, the welfare of whole communities. Natives were thus motivated to seek compromise and accommodation with an invader willing—and often able—to keep fighting until such an accommodation was reached. Indigenous leaders could not possibly have known that such compromises would result in three centuries of Spanish colonial rule.

Chapter 5
A shortcut to the grave

"The armies withdrew, each company back to its own garrison," wrote a veteran of conquest battles in South America. With a claim to true grit and grim bravado characteristic of these firsthand accounts, the conquistador added that "I went on to Nacimiento, which despite its fine name is nothing more than a shortcut to the grave—and there again I all but ate, drank, and slept in my armor."

The memoir continues with an account of how a Spanish force of five thousand was quartered on the plains, under constant attack from native warriors, "with everything but discomfort in short supply." Several times the Spaniards rode out to engage "the Indians," each time "gaining the upper hand and butchering them." But when native reinforcements arrived, "they killed many of our men, captains, my own lieutenant, and rode off with the company flag." Three of the conquistadors then took off on horseback after the flag, "trampling and slashing away" through "a great multitude of Indians." One Spaniard fell, but the other two overtook the flag:

> But then my other companion went down, spitted on a lance. I had taken a bad blow to the leg, but I killed the chief who was carrying the flag, pulled it from his body and spurred my horse on, trampling and killing and slaughtering more men than there are numbers— but badly wounded, with three arrows in me and a gash from a lance in my left shoulder which had me in great pain—until at last I reached our own lines and fell from my horse.

At first this memoir reads like a passage from the probanza of a sixteenth-century Spanish conquistador. Upon closer reading, it lacks any sort of self-reflective justification, the violence is recounted with a tad too much relish (one is reminded almost of Aguirre and his proud confessions of slaughter), and it has a swashbuckling air to it (much more so than most probanzas, even more than Bernal Díaz's narratives). But the account could nonetheless pass as a piece of conquistador petition-writing. Indeed, it is translated from a Spanish account penned by a conquistador. The twist is that the conquistador in question was not a sixteenth-century man, but a seventeenth-century woman— Catalina de Erauso—who escaped from a Basque nunnery in 1599 and in 1603 crossed to the Indies dressed as a man. There she lived for two decades as a latter-day conquistador, until she was exposed as a transvestite outlaw. Erauso was sent back to Spain, where she became an international celebrity, meeting both king and pope.

Imagining conquistadors

What better symbol of the shift in conquistador culture than Erauso's half-celebration, half-parody of the conquering Indies lifestyle? How does Erauso manage to get away with her gender-bending deception, acclaimed rather than condemned in the wake of her exposure? Is it because, as she herself claims, she remained a virgin? Or was it that by the 1620s—a century after the stunning news of the discovery and fall of the Aztec Empire had spread through Europe—Spaniards were in no mood for conquistador bashing?

If the latter explanation was true, one man, long dead by the 1620s, had much to do with it. Bartolomé de las Casas had arrived in the Americas a century before Catalina de Erauso. Las Casas was as much a symbol of those early Caribbean years as Catalina was a symbol of the overblown complexity of latter-day conquistador culture. Bartolomé's father had traveled as a merchant from Seville on one of the Columbus crossings of the 1490s and was grateful to have his son join him in the business of supplying the conquistadors invading the islands of the Caribbean. There the young Las Casas was a witness to, and participant in, the heady early days of opportunity and disappointment.

But from the onset of the conquest, among the merchants, captains, settlers, and priests, there were Spaniards who took more than a passing interest in the people and places they encountered. Some conquistadors observed their surroundings with sharp eyes, wrote about them, argued with their peers; a few of them took it to extremes. No doubt to his father's chagrin, Bartolomé de Las Casas's interest in the Taino led him out of the family business and into the priesthood. He renounced the trappings of settler success (his encomiendas on Cuba and Hispaniola) and became a Dominican firebrand, devoting his long life to a campaign to convince the king to make priests, not conquistadors, the governors of the new colonies. His experimental model settlements in Guatemala and Venezuela came to nothing, and the Spanish empire never became an archipelago of utopian religious colonies.

Las Casas's defense of Native Americans did not fall on deaf ears. He provoked such controversy that the king was obliged to listen. His arguments that native peoples be exempt from slavery, and that encomiendas (which provided Spaniards with native labor) not be passed on as inheritance by their Spanish holders, were reflected in a 1542 set of edicts known as the New Laws. Despite resistance and even rebellion from the conquistadors over the New Laws, they had a lasting impact on the development of the colonies. Las Casas's *Brief Account of the Destruction of the Indies* became a bestseller in his own lifetime. Until his death in 1566 he enjoyed the protection of the Crown and the right to petition in print and at court against abuses by the colonists against the colonized.

Las Casas was not an anti-imperialist nor a humanitarian or human rights activist in the modern sense. He did not denounce the Spanish empire or question its right to colonize. But he did oppose and denounce the methods of those who forged the empire; he attacked conquistadors and, in effect, the very essence of conquistador culture. Many of his writings, including the polemical *Brief Account*, were translated into other European languages and widely read by Spain's enemies. Las Casas's descriptions of conquistador atrocities became the foundation stones for the so-called Black Legend. Spanish imperialism was imagined in the Black Legend as excessively brutal and immoral. There were two ironies to the popularity of this depiction in Protestant countries. One was that the Protestant empires would themselves go on to match, and then exceed, the violence committed by Spanish American conquistadors. The other was the legend's implication that the Spanish were cruel because they were Catholic, ironic in view of Las Casas's insistence that the colonies should be run by priests.

There were as many Spaniards who loathed the *Brief Account* as there were Englishmen who loved it. One such hater was Bernardo de Vargas Machuca (see fig. 8). Born a few years after the *Brief Account* was first published, Vargas Machuca pursued a career as a latter-day conquistador in the final decades of the sixteenth century. In what is now Colombia, he ran punitive raids on "rebel" indigenous communities and hunted for the mythical jungle city of El Dorado. Fed up with the way in which Las Casas and his ilk ran down the conquistador reputation, in 1603 Vargas Machuca wrote a point-by-point refutation of Las Casas's accusations. Although his *Defense of the Western Conquests* was not published for centuries (first appearing in English in 2010), it captured some of the attitude toward what was coming to be seen as the golden age of the conquistador.

Viewed through Vargas Machuca's apologia, native peoples were so inherently savage and pugnacious that their conquest was in fact "pacification"—a term used by conquistadors from the earliest days of the conquest wars. Vargas Machuca turns the

Black Legend on its head, using the insulting adjectives that Las Casas threw at the conquistadors to describe "Indians": greedy, cruel, sexually depraved, cowardly. The classic conquistador figures are lauded in the predictable manner. For example, Machuca concluded, "God prepared, ordered, and guided the entry of don Hernando Cortés into New Spain." The conqueror of Mexico is portrayed as a profoundly religious nobleman, whose deeds were "courtly." Asks Vargas Machuca, "Why should this great gentleman and Christian deserve the title of cruel tyrant?"

Many Spaniards agreed, especially as the seventeenth century wore on; Vargas Machuca, it turns out, was ahead of his time. Although the century saw Las Casas's international reputation grow steadily, while Vargas Machuca's remained stillborn, the condemnation of conquistadors and their culture was neither taken for granted nor easily achieved in the Spanish world. It might be parodied, but in indirect ways. One example is Catalina de Erauso's picaresque memoir, with her exploits in South America as a form of performance parody. Another is Miguel de Cervantes's brilliant invention, the character of don Quixote de la Mancha, the ultimate delusional conquistador.

Yet for all the success of Cervantes's great novel, *The Ingenious Gentleman Don Quixote of La Mancha*, its eponymous protagonist was a conquistador who never left Spain. The ostensible target of the poet's wit was the knight of the age of chivalry, not the captain of conquest campaigns in the Indies; only very indirectly was don Quixote a Vargas Machuca or a Montejo, let alone a Cortés or an Aguirre. There are of course literary reasons why Cervantes chose to lampoon the chivalrous knight, rather than directly making the New World conquistador a farcical figure. But his choice is also explained by Spain's larger cultural and political context in the early seventeenth century. That context was not conducive to making mockery of the conquerors, even less so by the end of the seventeenth century.

For example, a look at the portraiture of the period reveals that conquistadors were eager to be seen on canvas as regal, dignified, and authoritative—a far cry from Cervantes's comical knight. Conquistador portraits drew inspiration and legitimacy from two other genres of portrait, the royal and the viceregal. Portraits of kings tended to set the visual tropes, which were then imitated in official portraits of Mexican and Peruvian viceroys, and in official and unofficial portraits of conquistadors. Vargas Machuca's imitation of Philip II's pose of a half century earlier (see fig. 8) was not simply a direct loan but part of a larger claim to status by association. Likewise, the half-length and three-quarter view of Jiménez de Quesada (see fig. 2) was a conventional pose of early modern painting, most notably that of official portraits of viceroys and governors of the empire's provinces. In Mexico City's royal palace, the seat of government for New Spain, there hung during the colonial centuries a series of half-length portraits of New Spain's viceroys—beginning with the first governor, Hernando Cortés.

A 1666 description of the portraits in Mexico City's royal palace also claims that Titian's famous painting of Charles V hung in the same room, sent to Mexico by the emperor "when he had the good news of the conquest of these kingdoms." That would have been an impossibility; the canvas must have been a copy of Titian's original, which was painted in 1548, two decades after word of the fall of the Aztecs reached Spain. No matter, the message was surely clear: king, viceroy, and conquistador were posed and juxtaposed in a relationship of legitimacy, authority, and loyalty.

The same message was displayed publicly in other paintings in the seventeenth century, most notably in dozens (perhaps scores) of serialized paintings depicting the Conquest of Mexico. Most of these series came in one of three formats: sets of between twenty and twenty-four panels, called *enconchados* ("shell-encrusted," after the mother-of-pearl mosaic around the edges); the sets of four to twenty folding screens called biombos (see fig. 3); and

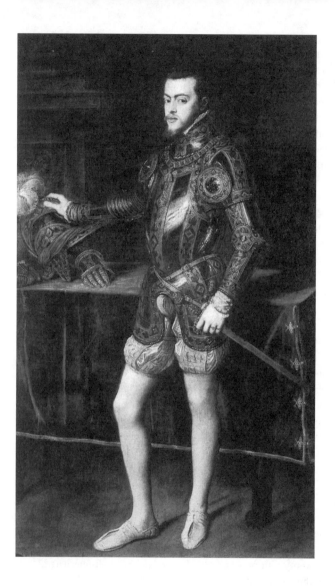

Text within image:

AMERICA

Nueva España

MAR DEL NORTE

P. DE CANCRO

EQVADOR

TROPICO D CAPRICOR

Peru

Chile

TERRA AVSTRALI. INCOGNITA

A la Espada y el compas
Mas y mas y mas y mas

8. Philip II and Bernardo de Vargas Machuca. The frontispiece to
don Bernardo de Vargas Machuca's *Indian Militia and Description of
the Indies*, published in Madrid in 1599 (*above*). The veteran of South
American conquest campaigns and apologist for the entire enterprise of the
Spanish Conquest appears to imitate the pose of the Spanish king Philip II
in the influential Titian portrait of 1551 (*opposite*).

sets of narrative paintings (such as the Kislak series, a set of eight wall-hung canvases). For decades scholars viewed such images as expressions of Mexican proto-nationalism. But recently the art historian Michael Schreffler has persuasively argued that "their representation of the narrative [of the conquest] glorifies (rather than displaces) the authority of the Spanish monarchy in New Spain." The popularity of Conquest of Mexico painting did not anticipate the resistance to imperial control of later centuries but was instead evidence of the increasing appropriation of the conquest and its conquistadors by Spanish imperialism.

The heyday of all this art—the enconchados, biombos, and wall paintings—was the late seventeenth century. For decades they served as visual siblings to the triumphalist versions of conquest history then in vogue. Most notable and influential among these was the official, new version of the Conquest of Mexico written by Philip IV's and Charles II's cronista del rey, Antonio de Solís y Rivadeneyra. First published in 1684, Solís's *History of the Conquest of Mexico* began with an attack on earlier historians of the Spanish Conquest, in whose writings he found "great daring and no less malice in the invention of whatever they wanted against the Spaniards, spending entire volumes citing the errors committed by some in order to discredit the achievements of all."

In glorifying Cortés and the heroic deeds of his fellow captains and "soldiers," Solís paid lip service to the conquistador spirit of individual initiative and enterprise. But the individualism that in reality lay at the heart of conquistador culture was ultimately buried by Solís, obscured beneath his recasting of the conquest as the achievement of Charles V and the direct manifestation in the New World of his empire. Conquistador culture in the sixteenth century had always nourished a thinly veiled disdain for imperial authority, a potential for disloyalty that sat on the thin line between the bitterness and crankiness of Bernal Díaz and Vargas Machuca, and the brute rebelliousness of Gonzalo Pizarro and Lope de Aguirre.

That tension was gone from the story by time it was told by Solís. It was also absent when Spaniards of the day laid claim to the conquistador legacy. An example is don Martín de Ursúa y Arizmendi, a Basque nobleman who came from a long line of conquistadors and who ended his career as governor of the Philippines (dying there in 1715). Ursúa would have read Solís's history in the late 1680s, when he was an ambitious lawyer and colonial official in Mexico City. By 1692, when he was appointed governor of Yucatan, he had conceived of a plan to follow in Cortés's footsteps and conquer the Itzá Maya.

The Itzá kingdom had survived and prospered, since Cortés had passed through it in 1525, in the tropical forests between the Spanish colonies in Yucatan and highland Guatemala. Ursúa told the king in 1692 that its "pacification" would be "the most glorious undertaking for the service of God and of Your Majesty in which I can employ myself." In the tradition of the original conquistadors, that of the era of his ancestor Pedro de Ursúa (who met a violent death in Peru in 1560), don Martín insisted that the campaign would be financed privately. It would cost the king nothing; the Crown's role would be to reward Ursúa with appropriate titles and lucrative positions once he had augmented the royal domain. In the words of his modern-day historian Grant Jones, "Ursúa saw himself, in effect, as a latter-day conquistador."

Ursúa was a wannabe Cortés. He was a conquistador in letter but not in spirit. He was a privileged bureaucrat who knew how to work the imperial system. He risked little, networked skillfully, rose profitably through the ranks. His business partner in Campeche had a brother on the Council of the Indies. He married a wealthy heiress of conquistador stock in Yucatan and used her fortune to fund his Itzá conquest. He mercilessly milked Yucatan's Maya population, pushing to punishing new levels the system of economic exploitation developed by his predecessors, and used the profits to buy himself the title of Count of Lizárraga. His career featured the conquistador characteristics of self-promotion and personal ambition, but without the suffering and sacrifice, without the rough edge of potential disappointment and disloyalty. Ursúa's ancestor Pedro had been killed in the Peruvian Amazon by other Spaniards, the sort of fate that was never in the cards for don Martín.

Latter-day conquistadors

The conquistadors have been portrayed as an overwhelmingly Spanish phenomenon, as indeed they were. Even the black and indigenous conquistadors were such because they operated within a Spanish American milieu. But conquistadors were part of a larger phenomenon of exploration, invasion, conquest, and colonization in the Americas. Can it be argued, then, that the conquistadors were merely the initial manifestation of a pattern of foreign invasion stretching from the first Atlantic crossings to the present? Should don Martín de Ursúa, as a latter-day conquistador, be seen as a final echo of the original conquistadors, as a coda to conquistador culture—or was he an early example of a latter-day conquistador culture that lasted for centuries? Is conquistador culture part of an ongoing phenomenon of conquest in the Americas, extending from Columbus and Cortés to the British and French, from Alaska to Patagonia, from the Mexican-American War to the Falklands/ Malvinas War? Have Europeans and Euro-Americans been trying to subject Native Americans for the past five centuries?

These larger arguments can certainly be made, and they reflect the broad brushstrokes of New World history. But they depend on generalizations and generous dollops of rhetoric, and they ignore the centrality of individualism to conquistador culture. One might step sideways—rather than forward—to look at the activities of the English, Scots, French, and other Europeans in the Americas in the sixteenth and seventeenth centuries, and thereby better understand conquistadors in the Spanish world. Such comparisons are outside the scope of this book, but they have started to be made successfully by scholars of empire in the early Americas. Yet there is a catch: the nation-state was rapidly growing within these empires, and after the sixteenth century it is increasingly the state that is formulating and guiding "conquest" activities. In the centuries leading to the present, such activities are overwhelmingly interventions, invasions, outright wars, covert wars, or proxy wars waged by national governments.

To find examples of individuals who might arguably be characterized as latter-day or modern-day conquistadors, we must look to the margins, not the mainstream, of the history of the Americas. There we find men like the infamous "filibuster" William Walker. As an individual with ambition and vision, not as a representative of the U.S. government, Walker raised funds and recruited men for conquest expeditions in Mexico and Central America. Like a sixteenth-century conquistador claiming territories that were intended to become provinces of Spain's empire, Walker carved new republics that were supposed to become states of the United States. He marched into Baja California with forty-five men in 1853, founding what he called the Republic of Lower California. That largely imaginary state was followed in 1854 by the Republic of Sonora and, two years later, by Walker's Republic of Nicaragua.

Walker has been studied as an odd example—even exemplum—of nineteenth-century U.S. imperial desire, of Manifest Destiny run amok, and of the development of modern American manhood. He was not unique in his time; there were at least a dozen other filibusters and freebooters engaged in similar enterprises in mid-century Mexico, Central America, and Cuba. But it is hard to miss the conquistador parallels. As Brady Harrison, a scholar of Walker's legacy in American literature and film, has commented, the "King of the Filibusters" was a "curious, and vicious, conquistador"—a description that could be applied to many a sixteenth-century Spaniard.

Walker repeatedly pronounced "himself president of a republic that did not exist in a territory that he did not control" (in Harrison's words), just as Cortés and his compatriots had three centuries earlier created town councils for nonexistent towns, founded cities in imaginary colonies, and invented titles of rulership over native kingdoms that they had not subdued. The difference is that Walker became a symbol of foreign policy gone awry, whereas Cortés became a symbol of imperial triumph. Walker's republic remains a chimera. Thousands of Americans did not settle Nicaragua, and the U.S. government in Washington did not confirm him in office as governor of a new state of the union. What sealed the fate and legacy of Cortés as being different from that of William Walker—or of Lope de Aguirre—was less the actions of these men and more the impact of the compatriots and imperial institutions that followed them.

Conclusion

In 1553, a group of several dozen black slaves was shipwrecked off the coast of what is now Ecuador. They washed ashore, bereft, bedraggled, and with little or nothing in the way of weapons or supplies. Alonso de Illescas rapidly assumed the leadership of the castaways. He had been a slave in Seville, where he acquired Christianity and the rudiments, at least, of Spanish culture. Within a matter of months, he established a privileged relationship with the local native chief, whose daughter he married and whose heir he became. Before he succeeded to the chieftaincy, he and his companions helped the locals in their wars against neighboring tribes and acted in effect as the chief's bodyguards.

The Spanish colonists in Quito—the nearest Spanish American city—strove for an understanding with "the black king of the Indians," as they called him. At times they sent diplomatic missions to try to get his assent for a road from Quito to the port he controlled, and at others they sent armies in unsuccessful attempts to enforce compliance. Illescas obtained the title of governor for the king of Spain, and ostentatiously flourished the dignity, without sacrificing any of his independence.

The little state he created broke up after his death into a number of petty "kingdoms" ruled by descendants of his black lieutenants. In 1599, in Quito, the painter Andrés Sánchez Gallque portrayed one of them, don Francisco de Arove, with his sons, on the occasion of his visit to be invested with the rank of royal governor (see fig. 9). The three black officials are sumptuously attired, in the height of aristocratic fashion, with ruffs so luxurious that in Spain the strict sumptuary laws would have forbidden them. In their ears and noses they wear golden ornaments of the kind that local natives reserved for the adornment of their rulers and the depiction of their gods. Within a few years, officials in Quito were complaining that the black officials remained as intractable and recalcitrant as ever. Their little kingdoms survived, effectively independent, for many generations.

The story resembles, in miniature, those of other—better known, Spanish, even famous—conquistadors. Strangers arrive, with no

9. The black conquistadors of Esmeraldas. Don Francisco de Arove, age fifty-six, with his two sons, don Pedro, age twenty-two, and don Domingo, eighteen years old, painted and signed by a Quito artist, Andrés Sánchez Gallque, in 1599 for Philip III, identified as "King of Spain and the Indies." The three maroon leaders are holding iron-tipped palm-wood lances, adorned with gold jewelry, wearing doublets, ponchos, silk capes, and white ruffs—all a combination of cloth and cut from China, Europe, and the Andes.

obvious advantages that might seem to destine them for power. They make themselves useful by virtue of the stranger-effect: their independence from traditional native factionalism makes them ideal in the roles of chiefly bodyguards and elite marriage partners. Their prowess in battle makes them enviable as allies. They exercise the influence of valued arbitrators. Indigenous society welcomes them with hospitality and rewards them with tribute, with services, and ultimately with power. They supply an additional level of leadership, supplementing or substituting or superimposed on traditional elites, rather than entirely displacing existing structures. Their success does not flow from superior weaponry, or horses, or any identifiable intellectual or moral advantage, or from the delusions of natives who mistook them for gods. On the contrary, it springs from well-disposed elements in native culture.

The trajectory to power of don Francisco de Arove and his colleagues was that of many or most of the Spanish conquistadors whose careers they seem to ape or mock. They, too, are conquistadors, and, perhaps, are as representative in their way as any of those whom the historical record has privileged—from the obvious Spaniards, such as Cortés and Pizarro, to the less obvious ones, such as Ursúa and Vargas Machuca. The category of conquistador is larger still, including such unconventional protagonists as Catalina de Erauso and don Francisco de Montejo Pech. Only by viewing the category as inclusive, and by appreciating the expansive nature of conquistador culture in the Americas, can we fully understand the conquistador phenomenon, the Spanish Conquest, and Latin American civilization.

Further reading

This bibliographic essay features only works in English, includes the major published sources used in the writing of this book and available in translation (but no untranslated works or unpublished archival sources), and leans toward more accessible editions and studies.

One example of a further introduction to or general history of the conquistadors, beyond this book, is Matthew Restall's *Seven Myths of the Spanish Conquest* (New York: Oxford University Press, 2003). John Pohl's *The Conquistador, 1492–1550* (Oxford: Osprey, 2001), aimed at school and undergraduate readers, is well informed and illustrated. Large, accessible histories of the rise of the Spanish Empire that give considerable attention to the conquistadors in the Americas include Henry Kamen's *Empire: How Spain Became a World Power, 1492–1763* (New York: HarperCollins, 2004) and the readable but old-fashioned "Spanish Empire Trilogy" by Hugh Thomas (*Rivers of Gold*, 2003, and *The Golden Age*, 2010, are the two volumes published to date), as well as his earlier *Conquest: Cortes, Montezuma and the Fall of Old Mexico* (New York: Simon & Schuster, 1995). Spanish explorations and conquests are placed in hemispheric and global contexts, respectively, in Felipe Fernández-Armesto's *The Americas: A Hemispheric History* (Random House, 2003) and *Pathfinders: A Global History of Exploration* (New York: Norton, 2006); also of relevance are a number of books by Fernández-Armesto on aspects of this topic, including *Columbus* (1991, but available in various editions), *1492: The Year the World Began* (New York: HarperOne, 2009), and *Amerigo: The Man Who Gave His Name to America* (New York: Random House, 2007).

On Native America on the eve of the conquest, see Charles C. Mann, *1491: New Revelations of the Americas Before Columbus* (New York: Knopf, 2005) for a masterful overview; and for more specific surveys, see Terence N. D'Altroy's *The Incas* (2003) and Michael E. Smith's *The Aztecs* (2002), both in Wiley-Blackwell's Peoples of America series, and David Webster's *The Fall of the Ancient Maya: Solving the Mystery of the Maya Collapse* (New York: Thames & Hudson, 2002).

The discussion of Jiménez de Quesada is drawn from the best book on his 1536–39 expedition, J. Michael Francis, *Invading Colombia: Spanish Accounts of the Gonzalo Jiménez de Quesada Expedition of Conquest* (University Park: Penn State University Press, 2007). This is the first volume in the Latin American Originals series; the first four books in the series offer new perspectives on the Spanish Conquest, and all have been used in the writing of this book. The other three are Matthew Restall and Florine Asselbergs, *Invading Guatemala: Spanish, Nahua, and Maya Accounts of the Conquest Wars* (2007); Carlos A. Jáuregui, *The Conquest on Trial: Carvajal's Complaint of the Indians in the Court of Death* (2008); and Kris Lane, *Defending the Conquest: Vargas Machuca's Apologetic Discourses* (2010).

Several fine editions of primary sources written by conquistadors and other Spaniards, published in translation, were used here. The classic edition of Bernal Díaz del Castillo's narrative is *The Conquest of New Spain* (New York: Penguin, 1963), but more useful is *The History of the Conquest of New Spain*, edited by Davíd Carrasco (Albuquerque: University of New Mexico Press, 2009). Also recommended are James Lockhart and Enrique Otte, *Letters and People of the Spanish Indies* (Cambridge: Cambridge University Press, 1976); Hernán Cortés, *Letters from Mexico*, edited by Anthony Pagden (New Haven, CT: Yale University Press, 1986); Catalina de Erauso, *Lieutenant Nun: Memoir of a Basque Transvestite in the New World*, translated by Michele and Gabriel Stepto (Boston: Beacon, 1996); Pedro de Cieza de León, *The Discovery and Conquest of Peru*, edited by Alexandra Parma Cook and Noble David Cook (Durham, NC: Duke University Press, 1998); Bartolomé de Las Casas, *An Account, Much Abbreviated, of the Destruction of the Indies*, edited by Franklin Knight, translated by Andrew Hurley (Indianapolis, IN: Hackett, 2003); Bernardo de Vargas Machuca, *The Indian Militia and Description of the Indies*, edited by Kris Lane, translated by Timothy Johnson (Durham, NC: Duke University Press, 2008).

There are also in print English translations of other Spanish accounts written in the sixteenth century, focusing entirely or partially on conquest events. These include accounts by friars—whose concern is mostly with the Spiritual Conquest, such as Diego Durán, Diego de Landa, and Toribio Motolinia—and accounts both by conquistadors, such as Juan de Betanzos, Alvar Núñez Cabeza de Vaca, and Pedro Pizarro, and Spanish chroniclers who did not fight in the New World, such as Francisco López de Gómara and Agustín de Zárate.

English translations of native accounts of the conquest wars (some written originally in Spanish, others in various indigenous languages) include Stuart B. Schwartz, ed., *Victors and Vanquished: Spanish and Nahua Views of the Conquest of Mexico* (Boston: Bedford/St. Martin's, 2000), which neatly juxtaposes Spanish accounts, chiefly that of Bernal Díaz (in the superior Maudslay translation), with Nahua and other native accounts, in the superior James Lockhart translation, the full text of which can be found in his *We People Here: Nahuatl Accounts of the Conquest of Mexico* (Berkeley: University of California Press, 1993); and Matthew Restall, *Maya Conquistador* (Boston: Beacon Press, 1998), which presents Maya accounts of the Conquest of Yucatan (and is used in our book here as the basis for comments on Yucatec Maya perspectives). A selection of primary sources relevant to this book is in chapter 1 of Matthew Restall, Lisa Sousa, and Kevin Terraciano, *Mesoamerican Voices: Native-Language Writings from Colonial Mexico, Oaxaca, Yucatan, and Guatemala* (Cambridge: Cambridge University Press, 2005). A Nahua historian, Domingo Francisco Chimalpahin Cuauhtlehuanitzin, wrote his own version in the early seventeenth century of López de Gómara's account of the Conquest of Mexico; it was recently published in English for the first time as *Chimalpahin's Conquest*, edited by Susan Schroeder et al. (Stanford, CA: Stanford University Press, 2010). There are two fine recent editions in English of an Inca account of the Conquest of Peru, that of Diego de Castro Yupanqui: one by Ralph Bauer, *An Account of the Conquest of Peru* (Boulder: University Press of Colorado, 2005); the other by Catherine Julien, *History of How the Spaniards Arrived in Peru* (Indianapolis: Hackett, 2006).

There are many accessible secondary works on aspects of the Spanish Conquest. Of note among them are Inga Clendinnen's *Ambivalent Conquests: Maya and Spaniard in Yucatan, 1517–1570* (Cambridge: Cambridge University Press, 2nd ed., 2003), which pairs well with

Restall's *Maya Conquistador*; Grant Jones's study of the Spanish destruction of the Itzá, *The Conquest of the Last Maya Kingdom* (Stanford, CA: Stanford University Press, 1998); and Anna Lanyon's books, *Malinche's Conquest* and *The New World of Martin Cortes* (originally published in Australia by Allen & Unwin, in 2000 and 2004 respectively). A more scholarly but still readable study of the historical doña Marina/Malinche is in Frances Karttunen's *Between Worlds: Interpreters, Guides, and Survivors* (New Brunswick, NJ: Rutgers University Press, 1994). A recent study of Spanish invasions into western Mexico is Ida Altman, *The War for Mexico's West: Indians and Spaniards in New Galicia, 1524–1550* (Albuquerque: University of New Mexico Press, 2010). Conquest studies emphasizing native roles and perspectives include Stephanie Wood, *Transcending Conquest: Nahua Views of Spanish Colonial Mexico*, and the essays in *Indian Conquistadors: Indigenous Allies in the Conquest of Mesoamerica*, edited by Laura Matthew and Michel Oudijk, both published by the University of Oklahoma Press (2003 and 2007). See, too, Serge Gruzinski's various studies, most notably his *Painting the Conquest: The Mexican Indians and the European Renaissance* (Paris: Flammarion, 1992). Also of use here was Michael Schreffler's study of *The Art of Allegiance: Visual Culture and Imperial Power in Baroque New Spain* (University Park: Penn State University Press, 2007). For more on how the Conquests of Mexico and Yucatan fit into the history of apocalypse, see Matthew Restall and Amara Solari, *2012 and the End of the World: The Western Roots of the Maya Apocalypse* (Lanham, MD: Rowman & Littlefield, 2011).

On the Andes and other South American regions, including discussion of the Esmeraldas maroons, we especially recommend *Quito 1599: City and Colony in Transition* by Kris Lane (Albuquerque: University of New Mexico Press, 2002). Kris Lane is also the premier historian of Vargas Machuca and his world, and Lane's insights in the two Vargas Machuca volumes listed above have been drawn upon in this book. John Hemming's *The Conquest of the Incas* was originally published in 1970 but remains a gripping read (available in various editions). James Lockhart's *The Men of Cajamarca: A Social and Biographical Study of the First Conquerors of Peru* (Austin: University of Texas Press, 1972) is still the best, detailed collective biography of any conquest expedition. An accessible introduction to Francisco Pizarro's life is Stuart Stirling, *Pizarro: Conqueror of the Inca* (Stroud, UK: Sutton, 2005). An important and useful scholarly study is Caroline A. Williams's *Between Resistance and Adaptation: Indigenous Peoples and the Colonisation in the Chocó, 1510–1753* (Chicago: University of Chicago Press, 2005). Stephen Minta's *Aguirre: The Re-creation of a Sixteenth-Century Journey Across South America* (New York: Henry Holt, 1994) is highly readable.

There is a substantial literature on Walker and his fellow filibusters, but of particular use here was Brady Harrison, *Agent of Empire: William Walker and the Imperial Self in American Literature* (Athens: University of Georgia Press, 2004) and Amy S. Greenberg, *Manifest Manhood and the Antebellum American Empire* (Cambridge: Cambridge University Press, 2005).

Finally, for more on the stranger-effect and an introduction to the relevant anthropological and sociological literature, see Felipe Fernández-Armesto, "The Stranger-effect in Early Modern Asia," in *Shifting Communities and Identity Formation in Early Modern Asia,* edited by Felipe Fernández-Armesto and Leonard Blussé (Leiden: Leiden University Press, 2003).

Index